NURTURING EFFECTIVE PARENT-TEEN COMMUNICATION AND LIFE SKILLS

EMPOWERED PARENT-TEEN CONNECTIONS:
NURTURING EFFECTIVE COMMUNICATION AND LIFE
SKILLS

SARAH HERMON

CONTENTS

INTRODUCTION

The easiest way to get your children to listen to you and to learn from you is by connecting with them first.

— CAROLINA KING

The teenage years are a strange and wonderful time for our children. During these years, they find themselves on the cusp of adulthood, which can be thrilling and unnerving. They are trying to understand their outer and inner worlds without giving in to the turmoil within them. During this time, they also tend to have a difficult relationship with their parents. On one hand, they want almost nothing to do with their parents because they want to start asserting themselves as adults. On the other hand, they need their parents more than ever because their first brush with adulthood can be confusing and unsettling at the best of times.

It makes sense, then, that this is a challenging time for parents as well. It's said that once you become parents, you must get used to having a piece of your heart outside you at all times. Now, as parents of teenagers, you get to see this piece of you make choices that can baffle you and even make you anxious. You might want nothing more than to take matters into your own hands and protect them from the business of living, but that wouldn't be fair to either of you, would it?

As parents, it's natural to see ourselves in our children. Sometimes, we might unknowingly impose our own desires and fears on them. As well-intentioned as we might be, we need to understand that our children are not a reflection of us or even an extension of us. In fact, they are their own people, even as they're trying to figure out who they are. Our role as parents is to give them the twin gifts of faith and support so that they can see and love themselves for who they truly are.

During this period, most parents find it challenging to communicate with their teenage children. Sometimes, we find ourselves in conflict with our children due to a clash in perspectives. Other times, we might want nothing more than for our children to share their concerns and confusion with us but are unable to bridge the gap between ourselves and them. No matter what we do, we might feel like we're not doing enough. Through this book, I want to make parents see beyond their helplessness and give them hope that a better relationship with their teenage children is possible.

Parents of teenagers want nothing more than to establish a strong bond with their children. They want to be able to help them navigate this challenging time of their life without taking away their autonomy in the process. As parents, we sometimes forget that our children also want the same thing. They want to connect with us, share their lives with us, and ask us for guidance when they're stumped. More often than not, we fail to sense this—especially as it might be cloaked in rebellion, anger, and resentment. When our teenagers are being "difficult," they're usually trying to find a way to make sense of their emotions and ask for help. Through this book, I hope to give you the tools required to truly listen to them.

This book is for any parent who wants to communicate effectively with their adolescent children, especially when it comes to matters of stress reduction and building resilience. Through this book, I want to help you understand your children better and understand what it means to be a teenager in today's world. This book will also help you have deeper and more meaningful conversations with your children and understand them better during this phase of their lives. Not only that, but you will also learn how to manage conflicts in a healthy manner and to use them to build a stronger relationship with your children. Last but not least, this book will help you with the tools needed to support your teenagers as they transition into adulthood—not only by giving them the knowledge and skills required to navigate this world but also by striking the right balance between autonomy and guidance in your relationship with them.

This book is divided into three parts. In the first part, we will try to truly understand our teenagers. We'll focus on the developmental changes that a teenager goes through during this period. We'll also discuss ways to connect deeply with our teens through effective and non-judgmental communication. The second part of this book deals with preparing our children for the world. We'll do this by learning about emotional intelligence, conflict resolution, and important life skills for our children. In the last part of the book, we will discuss all about mindful and gentle parenting. The aim is to be the kind of parents that our children can trust and be vulnerable with. Some of us need to work through our own past programming to become the parents that we never had. Others of us need to become less anxious when dealing with our children. Almost all of us need to breathe and anchor ourselves in the present so that we can become our children's anchors and safe harbors during this tumultuous period of their lives.

This book will help you challenge any toxic family dynamics in your life and replace them with healthier and happier dynamics. Hopefully, by the end of this book, you'll gain the confidence required to become a loving presence in your teenager's life. This is a time of numerous changes, so why not use it as an opportunity to create something lasting with your child? With this book by your side, you can let them know that—no matter what—they'll always have you by their side.

1

YOUR TEENAGER

For a parent, the teenage years of their child can be extremely challenging for a number of reasons. For one, their child is now at a unique stage in their life—not quite a child and not yet an adult. As such, they grapple with their own identity and try to understand what they stand for. At the same time, they undergo so many changes—emotional, physical, hormonal, and cognitive—during this period of time that it can be overwhelming for both them and their parents. What's more, these changes—which are challenging enough on their own—don't happen in a vacuum. This is a period where your teen is constantly being shaped by their familial and social environment. These interactions play a huge role in determining their mental, emotional, and even physical health.

When we're struggling to understand our teenagers, we must not lose sight of the fact that they're going through the same process. They want to understand themselves and the world around them, but their brain is frequently overwhelmed by everything they need to deal with. This is why it might sometimes feel like you and your teenager are speaking two different languages. To form a strong bond with your teen, you need to become fluent in their language and understand the world they inhabit at the moment. In this chapter, we'll try to do exactly that.

THE ADOLESCENT BRAIN: A NEUROLOGICAL JOURNEY

Many researchers have tried to understand how the brain develops during adolescence. This results in multiple theories, many of which challenge how we traditionally view brain development in adolescents. In a paper that was published in *Nature*, a few of these studies and their conclusions were discussed. A very interesting point made by researchers is that, while a teenager might seem like an adult in many ways—and would certainly want to be treated as one—their brain is not ready in terms of cognitive ability.

What does this mean? It means that most behaviors that are easy for adults aren't really easy for teenagers. For example, many teenagers have to exert a lot of effort in order to control their impulses, something that is usually easier for adult brains. This is also one of the reasons why teens might be more prone to risk-taking behaviors. Another important aspect of a teen's cognitive development is *neuroplasticity*. Neuroplasticity is the ability of our brains to form new neural pathways and erase old ones, thus creating significant new connections that help us grow and evolve cognitively. Now, neuroplasticity isn't something that happens only in teenage brains. In fact, if we start a new habit and keep at it for some time—or if we meditate consistently for a longer period of time—we can avail ourselves of the benefits of neuroplasticity at any age. With teens, however, this happens in an almost automatic manner as their brains are still developing at a rapid pace. This is why your teen could actively seek new experiences all the time.

Neuroplasticity occurs through a process known as "synaptic pruning." During this process, the grey matter present in the brain starts thinning as unnecessary nerve cell connections are gotten rid of to make way for those that are more relevant to your teenager's brain. What does this mean for them and you? It means you can play a role in how their brain develops during this time. The environment you provide for them will influence which characteristics or behaviors become predominant in them during this age. This is a time when you can expose them to various interesting activities and environments, which can help them develop new skills and direct their energy in a productive manner.

Another aspect of the neurological development of our teens is that this period sees their prefrontal cortex starting to develop. At the same time, their reward center is overstimulated. The prefrontal cortex is the region of the brain responsible for regulating our thoughts, feelings, and actions. During adolescence, this region isn't fully developed, which means that many teens have issues with emotional and mental regulation at this time. What's more, some teens can face greater problems than others, meaning some might find it more difficult to keep their emotions and impulses in check.

At the same time, this is a period when the reward center of our brain gets lit up every time we perform an activity that brings us pleasure. In order for a habit to fully form, our reward center needs to light up when we perform that activity. This provides the brain with the necessary feedback to keep repeating the action, thus eventually forming a habit. Now, in teenagers, the need to experience a "high"—which is the equivalent of the reward center being flooded with feel-good hormones—is much more pronounced. This is why our teenagers might be actively involved in various thrill-seeking behaviors, which might not be the most prudent choice for them (Powell, 2006).

What does this mean for you? You can use these learnings to better understand your teenager during this exciting and confusing time:

- If your teenager is impulsive or doesn't know when to say "no," they're not doing this to trouble you or to be rebellious. Consider that they might genuinely find it difficult to control their impulses during this time.
- The fact that their brain undergoes synaptic pruning at this time offers an opportunity for you to direct them toward more enriching and meaningful activities. The aim is to keep them engaged in constructive ways.
- Understand that your teenager's brain does not work like an adult's or a child's during this time, which means there are fundamental differences between your way of thinking and theirs. This also means that you cannot always solve their problems rationally or by giving them a specific set of instructions to follow.
- The fact that your teenager craves more stimulation and rewards during this time

doesn't have to be a bad thing. Instead, it can encourage you to come up with activities that provide a positive outlet for their energy instead of letting them give in to dangerous behavior.

- Instead of seeing their behavior as challenging, disruptive, or willfully difficult, try to understand that they are wired in a way that is different from yours and that these changes are usually more overwhelming to them than they are to you.

EMOTIONAL DEVELOPMENT IN ADOLESCENCE

During adolescence, our children learn—perhaps for the first time—to manage their emotions on their own. If this wasn't challenging enough, adolescence is a period of huge emotional turmoil for most people. Think of it as someone who doesn't know how to swim being thrown into the deep end of the pool. That's a bit like what emotional development in adolescence can look like. There are various factors that can affect our teens' emotional development. Let's discuss some of these in this section.

The Impact of Hormones on Mood and Behavior

Adolescence is a period when our body starts producing various kinds of hormones that affect both our moods and behaviors. Specifically, the hypothalamus produces *gonadotropin*—a hormone that causes our pituitary gland to release growth, sex, and adrenal hormones. The primary female sex hormone is estrogen, while the male sex hormone is testosterone. The adrenal hormones consist of adrenaline and nora-drenaline. Most of these hormones are at their peak between the ages of 7-13 for girls and between the ages of 9-15 for boys (Breehl, 2023). However, not everyone will feel the effects of these hormones at the same time.

These hormonal changes not only affect our physical characteristics but also play a role in our mental and emotional health. As teens hit puberty, they have to deal with many changes in their bodies, which can be extremely confusing and overwhelming to deal with on their own. These hormones will also affect their sexual feelings and attraction toward others. These sex hormones can also affect our mental health. For example, high levels of estrogen (or low levels of testosterone) can lead to irritability, while low levels of estrogen can lead to low levels of serotonin—which has been linked to depression. Not only that, but when teens suffer from hormonal imbalances, they also have to deal with issues such as fogginess, anxiety, confusion, mood swings, and even social withdrawal.

Since their bodies also undergo changes at this time, it can be deeply unsettling for teens to come to terms with their appearance and physical health. This can lead to feelings of helplessness or isolation, especially in their peer groups. Sometimes, when these hormones are produced in overabundance, it can also lead to reckless behavior by teenagers.

We've discussed in the previous section how teenagers' reward centers can be more active than those of adults. This reward center is tied to hormones such as vasopressin, oxytocin, and dopamine. Among these, oxytocin and vasopressin are especially related to feelings of love and acceptance in both interpersonal and social settings. In other words, these hormones help make us feel safe, trusted, and part of the groups that matter to us. When there's an imbalance in these hormones, it can affect our social and personal relationships, as well as our emotional responses to these scenarios. In teenagers, these feelings are intensified, which means that these hormones affect everything from their social interactions to their romantic and platonic relationships.

The Effect of the Environment on Your Teen's Emotions

The teenage brain is affected heavily by environmental factors. On one level, teens tend to move away from the influence of parents and family and align themselves more closely with their peer groups. While this can help with their emotional development in some ways, it also brings with it various kinds of challenges that might overwhelm them every now and then. For one, they are faced with many kinds of emotions at this time, some of them contradictory to one another. They might also find that their emotions regarding the same thing or person differ from one moment to the next. There might be days when they feel like their emotions are betraying them.

Also, since teens want to assert their autonomy at this time, they also want to start making decisions on their own. The problem is they now have to deal with more uncertainties than ever before. They are coming to terms with the fact that there are very few definite answers in this world, which means they need to think in more abstract terms than before. They also need to balance logic with emotion while making decisions, which is extremely difficult when their emotions seem to overpower them. During this time, it matters immensely whether they feel seen and supported by their peers and parents. Even though they might make it seem like they don't *want* their parents' support at this time, it makes a world of difference to them if they have understanding and patient parents. While the best-case scenario is that they find a healthy peer group that makes them feel good about themselves, they need their parents to let them know that the world isn't going to end when things don't go their way.

Another reason why the environment matters a lot for your teen's emotional development is that they need help understanding all the changes they're undergoing at once. For instance, puberty brings with it hormonal changes and feelings related to romance and sex. Many teenagers—depending on cultural and familial factors —start dating for the first time at this age. Not only does this lead to a heady mix of confusion, excitement, and apprehension, but it also intensifies each of these feelings for them. This means that the feelings of "love" they experience might be overwhelming for them, and so would any feeling of rejection. If they experience insecurity or jealousy in their relationships, these feel-ings are also unusually strong.

It's one thing to experience such strong emotions as a teenager and another to feel isolated or misunderstood because of them. If teachers, parents, or even peers make them feel like they're "too much," it might cause them to shut down or blame themselves for their emotions. Therefore, it's important to provide them with an environment where they can freely express themselves and also communicate their feelings without judgment.

Identity Formation: Who Am I?

Adolescence is a period where identity formation starts in earnest. As teens begin to understand the world around them—and their place in it—they also come to terms with who they are and who they want to be in the future. There are two main aspects of identity that teens have to deal with—self-concept and self-esteem. While self-concept talks about how teens view themselves, self-esteem also takes into account how others view them (or how they think others view them). Your teen's self-concept can be related to their values, beliefs, and interests. Their self-esteem, on the other hand, is related to their social and interpersonal interactions, social media usage, and their treatment by their friends and family members.

There are various challenges that adolescents might face in terms of identity formation:

- **Identity is a fluid concept**, which means it can change from one moment to the next. Navigating these changes without feeling overwhelmed can be difficult for anyone, but more so for teenagers.

- **Not everyone has a strong self-concept**, which means that many struggle to know exactly who they are and what they stand for. This isn't a bad thing at all, but it can seem intimidating to navigate this world without a self-concept.
- **The pressure to find their identity** is immense, especially in the age of social media. Everyone must know who they are, and only then can they create and live up to their image in front of others.
- Their **self-esteem depends a lot on how others view them**, meaning that other people's perceptions can lead to both high and low self-esteem in adolescents. While people with a strong self-concept can combat feelings of low self-esteem, it takes a lot of willpower to do so.
- During this time, many teens experience **a conflict between figuring out their true identity and conforming to social and cultural ideals.** Since they want to fit in, it can be challenging to know who they truly are without the influence of peer pressure.

This process of identity formation can have a huge impact on the emotional and mental health of teenagers. Those who have a strong self-concept and high self-esteem usually know how to manage their emotions in a healthy manner. On the other hand, teens who feel misunderstood, misrepresented, or ostracized due to their identity—such as their sexual, cultural, and gender identity—face challenges related to their mental and emotional health. In extreme cases, this can even lead to mental health issues such as anxiety, depression, and eating disorders.

The Effect of Stress on Emotional Development in Teens

Adolescence is usually a stressful time for everyone involved. Teenagers—during this time—face the stress of figuring out their identities, finding groups they belong to, and deciding what they want to do with their lives. As they come to terms with a world that is rapidly changing—and a world where they need to assume responsibility for their own life—it's understandable that they experience stress from time to time.

It's also vital to point out that not all stress is harmful. For instance, if the stress of doing well academically prompts your teen to focus on your studies, it's a good thing. Similarly, the stress of figuring out their identity can encourage a teen to explore the world to under-stand themselves better. In other words, some stress might be essential for teenagers to grow as individuals. At the same time, when stress levels become too high, or when teenagers start stressing about things that impact them negatively, it takes a toll on their mental, emotional, and physical health.

This is also tied to the effect of hormones on their emotions. When there's too much stress in their lives, it leads to an increase in the stress hormone cortisol. At the same time, it triggers the fight-or-flight response of the body, which can interfere with sleep and also lead to anxiety and depression in some cases. Therefore, keep in mind where the stress is originating from. If it's related to the pressure of fitting in or to low self-esteem, then it's something that needs to be addressed as soon as possible.

Since this is a time of immense emotional and mental upheaval, it might be easy to ignore signs of stress. If your teenager has witnessed or experienced abuse or trauma of any kind—and they don't reach out for support—they might need to repress their feelings in order to present themselves as normal to the world. These repressed feelings can then lead to emotional withdrawal or to episodes of aggressive or risk-taking behavior. In some cases, teens might struggle with post-traumatic stress disorder—which might require profes-sional intervention.

Adolescence is a critical time for the development of emotional intelligence. On the one hand, teens need to become aware of their own as well as others' emotions. On the other hand, they need to be able to regulate their emotions in a healthy manner and also respond to other's emotions in a mature and sensitive way. These are difficult skills to master, and it may take a long time to become better at them—even as adults. At the same time, this is a period where we can help our kids add to their emotional arsenal through the very experiences that challenge them.

PEER INFLUENCE: FRIENDS AND FOES

We've discussed the importance of peer pressure in the emotional development of teenagers. In this section, we'll be discussing the concept of peer influence. As our teenagers move away from their families and try to understand themselves through their peer groups, the importance of the groups they belong to—as well as those they don't—increases manifold. The thing is, this effect isn't always negative, as it might seem when we use the term "peer pressure." Peer influence refers to the many ways in which our teenager's peer affect their quality of life.

On the positive side, their peer groups can make it easier for them to explore themselves. If they have supportive and encouraging friends, they might feel good about themselves, enjoy high self-esteem, and also be willing to take a chance on themselves. Teens who find acceptance in these groups are more confident about facing the world head-on. Generally, teens try to interact with people they have something in common with or from whom they want to learn something. The people they choose to be with have an effect on their attitudes and behaviors, both within and outside their group.

While the tendency to form groups or find commonalities with others is prevalent, it can also take an unhealthy turn if these groups are used to target or ostracize people. For example, if a certain person feels rejected by their group—or finds it difficult to form a group in the first place—they might suffer from low self-esteem, resentment, and self-criticism. If a teenager already belongs to a marginalized group in terms of race, sexuality, or gender—these issues can be exacerbated. When these experiences take on a darker turn—in the form of bullying, for example—they might damage our teenager's mental and emotional health.

While it can feel great for teenagers to be included by their peers, this acceptance can also come at a cost. For instance, if your teen needs to change something fundamental about themselves—or if they need to take part in risky activities—in order to become a part of a group, it's a matter of concern. This isn't limited to the groups they interact with physically. The impact of pop culture and media only adds to the pressure that teens feel to live a "happening" and "adventurous" life. They might feel pressured to follow the trends of the day or to be aware of everything that's happening around them. If they can resist the negative aspects of this culture and use it to explore themselves further, it results in an enriching and successful adolescence. However, many succumb to this pressure and deal with feelings of inadequacy and loneliness.

A study showed that peer pressure has a direct impact on negative body image in adolescents. While there are some cases of positive influence due to peers, the consequences are mostly negative in nature. What's more, both men and women feel the pressure to look a certain way in order to be accepted by their peers (Kenny et al., 2016). The trick lies in finding the balance between developing themselves as an individual and finding a group that helps them in positive and life-affirming ways. Teens who have faith in themselves—and who feel loved and respected for who they are by their parents—might find it easier to deal with the negative effects of peer influence.

THE ROLE OF SOCIAL MEDIA

Adolescence is challenging even without social media, as much of the story plays out in the presence of peer groups. Nevertheless, the use of social media comes with its own set of rules and behaviors—which can further complicate things for both teenagers and their parents. One thing that many researchers are now paying attention to is that social media might not be entirely negative for teenagers. In fact, social media might open up new avenues of exploration for teens and make it easier for them to understand themselves.

Here are a few ways in which the judicious use of social media can help teenagers:

- For teens who aren't able to express themselves freely in front of their parents, social media can provide a lot of resources and options to deal with the challenges of adolescence.
- Teens who struggle with making friends in person—either due to shyness or isolation—can be a part of online groups where they meet like-minded peers and where they can be themselves without judgment.
- Social media also provides an outlet for creative expression that might otherwise not be otherwise available to them.

- In many cases, social media can help combat feelings of loneliness by making them aware of the world around them, connecting them to others, and helping them feel understood.
- Social media also exposes teens to a world beyond their neighborhood. If used wisely, this can help them understand more of the larger world and develop empathy by coming across various viewpoints and ways of life.

According to a recent study, 43% of 1500 teen participants stated that social media helps them feel better when they're anxious or depressed. Similarly, 52% of the LGBTQIA+ participants reported that social media helps them feel less lonely when they're going through a difficult time (*The Common Sense Census: Media Use by Tweens and Teens, 2021*, 2022).

At the same time, excessive use of social media can have numerous negative effects on the mental and emotional health of teenagers. For instance, some researchers believe that those who use social media a lot have a higher chance of developing anxiety or depression. Some, however, believe that those who are anxious or depressed frequently use social media as an outlet for their thoughts and feelings. For example, when we feel rather helpless and depressed about the world, we might resort to "doomscrolling"—an activity where we endlessly scroll through our devices and keep getting bombarded by bad news. At the same time, doom-scrolling can lead to anxiety and depression in some of us. So, the question is, is social media use the cause or the symptom of poor mental health? As of now, it might be a bit of both.

Here are some negative effects of social media use on teenagers:

- Teens might sacrifice sleep or disrupt their usual sleeping patterns in order to maintain or increase their social media use.
- Poor sleep can also lead to changes in moods and behavior over a prolonged period of time.
- Social media use can also keep them from indulging in regular physical activity, thus leading to concerns about both mental and physical health.
- Social media can influence them to adopt more risky behaviors by making them seem aspirational.
- Since social media can provide us with distance and even masked identities, it can also lead to cyberbullying and toxic behaviors that cause a lot of harm to teenagers.

- Social media can lead to body image issues as well as exacerbation of depression, anxiety, and eating disorders.

While it might not be possible or advisable for you to restrict your teenager's social media use, you can certainly monitor it and have honest conversations with them about the challenges they might be facing as a result of it. It's also important to understand that your teen might not share their online life or their social media use with you, so you need to build trust and let them know that you can provide them a judgment-free space to ask for help if needed.

COGNITIVE MILESTONES IN TEENAGERS

When we hit adolescence, our minds start to work differently from when we were children. These changes don't occur overnight, and everyone experiences a different pace of cognitive development. Also, these changes don't occur in a vacuum meaning the environment in which your teen grows plays a huge role in their cognitive development.

Here are some of the cognitive milestones that your teenager might experience during this period:

- **They might move from concrete to abstract thinking:** Abstract thinking allows your teen to appreciate and work through the uncertainties of life. They learn to question things, understand that things don't work in binaries, and look deeper while dealing with issues. As they begin to form romantic and platonic relationships on their own—and also start thinking about a career for the first time—they begin to dream about the future and imagine the various possibilities in life. Abstract thinking might be challenging in the beginning, but it can help them immensely in thinking about various scenarios in their life.

- **They will learn to make better decisions in life:** During this period, teens need to balance their emotions with logic—making decisions that don't lead to devastating consequences. They also learn to deal with lots of information at one time, processing it and choosing the best course of action based on it. Of course, this also means that they make mistakes, but these mistakes can help them make better decisions in the future.

- **They will begin to entertain multiple points of view:** As teens begin to form their own opinions on various topics—especially political ones—they learn to widen their own horizons and listen to others. During this period, they need to respect diverse views while also gaining confidence in their own beliefs. Learning to debate and discuss topics that are important to them without letting their emotions get the better of them is a useful skill and one that parents can help teens learn.

- **They might question everything:** Adolescents are infamous for saying "no" to anything their parents might suggest and for questioning everything that is told to them. While this can be frustrating, it also indicates that teenagers are learning to think for themselves, and they're refusing to accept anything passively. If parents work with their teens during this time, they can help foster this spirit of independent thinking in them.

- **They can now think about thinking:** Known as *metacognition*, the process of understanding one's own thought processes at a deeper level is an extremely useful one. This trait helps teenagers become aware of their cognitive behaviors and come up with various techniques that can help them perform better in various aspects of their lives.

Now that we've understood how the teenage mind works, we can move on to effective communication techniques we can use to build a strong bond with our own teens.

2

BUILDING BLOCKS OF
EFFECTIVE COMMUNICATION

One of the biggest challenges any parent of teens faces is getting their teen to communicate with them. During this time, most of us consider ourselves lucky if our teen as much as acknowledges our presence in their lives. It can seem like they don't need us or our opinions, which makes it very difficult for us to have heartfelt conversations with them. While we do have our moments with them, they seem to happen almost miraculously, through no effort from us. How do we establish a bond with our kids and maintain communication with them during this time of their lives? How do we become a trusted presence for them to turn to when they want to be vulnerable and honest with someone? How do we truly listen to them and understand the unique challenges that they face at this time?

FROM SMALL TALK TO HEART-TO-HEART

On a good day, our teen might respond to our queries with more than a grunt or nod. Small talk is difficult for anyone, but trying to get our teens to talk to us without any agenda can be especially challenging. This is because they're usually glued to their screens or worrying about how to present themselves to their peer group. They're looking for acceptance and belonging in the families they're busy creating for themselves, so it can seem like they're not keen on having conversations with their own families.

Sometimes, their behavior might make us defensive, and we might react in a way that is not helpful to them. There are some things that we need to keep in mind if we want our teenagers to warm up to us and confide in us:

- **Don't take things personally:** I know this can seem like the hardest thing to do for most of us. I'm not saying it will never hurt us when our teenagers act standoffish around us. What helps me is remembering that I, too, was a teenager once. During that time, I wasn't trying to hurt my parents or to prove that I didn't need them anymore. Instead, my entire focus was on building my own identity and proving to myself that I could thrive in this world. Remembering my own struggles as a teen helps me empathize with my own teens, especially when they seem distant to me.

- **There's no gift like presence:** The thing with teenagers is that they're not always sure about when they need our presence. Even if they're rejecting us or distancing themselves from us on the surface, they might need us to check in with them and reassure them of our presence. This doesn't mean that we impose on them all the time. Instead, we can give them their space but also let them know that we're right here if they need us.

- **Be consistent with your teen:** Adolescence is a time when our teens are dealing with uncertainties of every kind. As such, their own behavior can sometimes be erratic. However, this is also when they need you to be their rock, even if they don't say it in so many words. So, when it comes to communication, make sure you're consistent in your tone and message as much as possible. This can make them comfortable sharing their thoughts and feelings with you.

- **Convince your teen that you are always in their corner:** You and your teen are not going to agree on everything. In fact, you'll be at loggerheads more than you would like. At the same time, it's imperative that your teen knows you're on their side, no matter what. Help them understand that even when you're fighting *with* them, you're truly fighting *for* them.

- **Keep in mind that what is trivial to you might not be trivial to them:** A teen's sense of scale is very different from their parents'. Many things that might seem like nothing to us could feel like a matter of life and death to our teens, which is why every conversation should be treated as important. Even when we're engaging in small talk or when they're "ranting" about their day to us—we need to appreciate the fact that they're communicating with us something that matters to them. When we treat their efforts with respect and consideration, we tell them that we're trying to understand them.

ACTIVE LISTENING: THE KEY TO UNDERSTANDING

Active listening is one of the most effective ways in which you can be present for your teen. As parents, we often have a tendency to help our kids out by giving advice or by weighing in with our own experiences and perspectives. These are helpful gestures, but only when our teens are receptive to them. For example, if our teens specifically ask us for information or advice (which is rare, I know!)—we should help them however we can. At the same time, if our kids simply want us to listen, pay attention to them, or work through their emotions in our presence—nothing can be more powerful than active listening.

Here are some vital points that will help you decide why and when you should practice active listening with your teen:

- **Active listening is a great way to center your teen's emotions and thoughts:** As an active listener, you're letting your own thoughts and opinions take a backseat to your teenager's. You're willing to hear them out and listen to what they want to say about a subject. As such, it also works very well in situations where you don't have a personal agenda. For example, if your teen wants to vent about something that has happened in his friend group, you can listen to them without letting your own emotions take over.

- **Active listening is all about giving your teen attention and showing faith in them:** When your teen confides something in you, you can either be preoccupied with your own thoughts, or you can give them your full attention. Either way, your teen will receive the message. By allowing them to talk about their experiences, you're not only telling them that their issues are important to you, but you're also letting them form their own thoughts and communicate them to you. It's an act of deep trust and one that your teen will be immensely thankful for.
- **Active listening is not about problem-solving, at least not for you:** In many cases, your teen simply needs to vent about their concerns for them to feel heard and understood. In some cases, they might need to come up with a solution to a problem, but this does not mean that you need to chip in unless specifically asked. I understand how difficult it can be not to help our child when that is all we want to do, but this is an opportunity for you to show them that you trust them. It's also a great way for

them to develop their own problem-solving skills.

- **There are certain situations where active listening is not useful:** Sometimes, you might need to take action, or your child might need you to intervene in a situation. Other times, it might simply not be possible for you to maintain an objective point of view in certain scenarios. These are some instances where active listening can defeat the purpose of the interaction. Also, since active listening requires that you listen calmly and attentively, it's also necessary for you to be in the proper frame of mind. If you're unable to give your teen the attention they deserve, it's not a bad idea to be honest with them. Otherwise, your reactions might end up doing more harm than good.

How to Practice Active Listening

Here are a few things you can keep in mind while trying to become an active listener for your teen:

- **Dedicate your time and attention to your teen:** I understand that it is not always possible. If you're very busy, explain to your teen that you want to give them the attention they deserve and schedule your interaction with them as early as possible. However, there will be times when your teen will need your immediate attention, and you should be able to set aside time for them. This is to let them know that whatever they have to say is significant to you. Also, make sure that you maintain gentle eye contact with them while they're talking to you. It's the easiest way to establish a connection with your teen, provided they are comfortable with it.

- **Keep your own emotions out of the equation as much as possible:** This is going to be difficult as a parent, especially if you feel like your child is in pain. Also, when our teens tell us something about their own experiences, it's normal to project our own feelings on them. This goes against the objective of active listening. During this time, your only aim is to listen to your child and let them make sense of their own feelings.

- **Respect your teen's feelings through words and gestures:** There are many ways to show your teen that you respect how they're feeling at this time. When you use words, make sure that you reflect their own words back to them in a thoughtful manner. For example, if your teen says, "I don't want to go to school as it doesn't interest me," you can reply with, "It must be difficult to feel excited about school if you feel like you're not learning anything new." Now, this is not the same as just repeating what your teen has said. You're acknowledging their frustration and also gently prodding them to tell you more. Likewise, your gestures should be empathetic at all times. For instance, if you think that your teen is worried about something that is "not a big deal," keep it to yourself and don't raise your eyebrows or roll your eyes. Most of the time, we don't even know that we're behaving this way, so you might need to consciously check yourself when interacting with your teen in the beginning.

- **Don't push them to tell you things or to talk any more than they want to**—When our teen decides to confide in us, we often feel so excited that we forget to keep in mind what they need from us. When we're engaging in active listening, we need to make sure that we're allowing them to communicate with us on their own terms. If you feel like your teen is unable to tell you something or that they're shutting down in some way, you should let them know that you're available when they need to talk.

NONVERBAL COMMUNICATION: BEYOND WORDS

When we're creating a safe space to bond with our teens, communication becomes the most powerful tool we have to do so. At the same time, most of this communication isn't even done verbally. There are two reasons for this. One, all of us express ourselves through nonverbal cues a lot more than we would like to believe. Two, our teens might find it difficult to communicate everything through words, which means that we should pay attention to their nonverbal cues while communicating with them. Nonverbal cues range from the tone of your voice to the gestures that you use and from your body language to your smile.

One thing to keep in mind is that our teens aren't able to process nonverbal cues as well as we can. This is because, while adults can analyze these cues through their prefrontal cortex, teens do so through their limbic system—which is responsible for their fight-or-flight responses. So, while adults are right about what certain nonverbal cues mean 90-100% of the time, teens are right only about 50% of the time (McNutt, 2017). How does this affect their interactions with those around them?

For starters, it makes the world highly confusing for them. Your teen might often have trouble interpreting what their parents or peers are trying to convey to them. This can lead to feelings of isolation and frustration. Not only that, but it can lead to a lot of problems with their peers, as they're all a bunch of teenagers who aren't sure of how to interpret nonverbal cues. As a parent, what you can do is encourage them to talk about how certain cues make them feel. For instance, if they feel upset after a conversation with you—and you don't remember *saying* anything unpleasant—you can always check in with them and ask them to label how they felt after seeing you and talking to you. This exercise can also help you become more conscious of your own nonverbal cues around them. At the same time, since you can process nonverbal cues much better than your teen, you can use it to your advantage when your teen isn't keen on talking to you.

When it comes to protecting our teens, we need to be especially mindful of what is known as "relational aggression." Our teens need validation and acceptance from their peer groups, but they can also feel isolated and targeted because of them. Some instances of bullying and harassment are more obvious than others. When it comes to relational aggression, the signs might be hard to spot for parents and harder for teens. Relational aggression occurs when people use covert tactics to make someone feel lonely or ridiculed. For instance, what happens when some members of your teen's friend group stop talking to them all of a sudden? Or when your teen hears that there have been rumors about them—even though they don't know the source of these rumors? The harder it is to point out *what* is wrong—for example, body language that isn't overtly hostile but neither is it friendly—the more challenging it can get your teen to pinpoint their concerns.

If you ever have a similar with your teen—and you find them stonewalling you or being unable to tell you why they're upset about something—don't dismiss them. Instead, understand that they're confused and that they might need to make sense of their own emotions. What this also means is that you need to let your teen tell you how they felt during an interaction, and you need to convince them that their feelings are valid.

CREATING SAFE SPACES FOR CONVERSATION

In the last section, we spoke about how our teens might need us to provide a safe space for conversations with them. Here are some things we can do to ensure we do so:

- **Our teens don't want judgment; they want our unconditional acceptance:** When we judge our teens, we make it difficult for them to open up to us. Instead, we need to show them that we love them unconditionally. It's also important to understand that we don't need to accept everything that our teens think or do. Instead, we need to let them know that we're on their side, even when we disagree about certain topics.

- **Create an atmosphere of trust and support:** When you ask your teenager questions, make sure they are kind and supportive in nature. Similarly, while you should verify certain things that your teen tells you, do it in a way that doesn't sound accusatory or presumptuous. Also, let them know that you're going to always believe in them so they can come to you with the truth.

- **Be careful with penalties:** You might have to penalize your teens for certain actions of theirs, but make sure that you don't punish them for coming to you with the truth. This can be extremely difficult to implement, especially if you don't communicate well with them. For instance, if your teen confides in you about having attended a party under false pretenses, you need to let them know that you appreciate them coming clean about it. Also, bring your focus to the reasons behind their betrayal instead of the betrayal itself. Like, ask them why they were unable to let you know before going to the party. Is it because they think you're unduly strict and unreasonable, or because they knew what they were asking for was problematic? Make sure that your teen understands they're not going to be penalized for being honest and open with you.

- **Let them know that you embrace imperfection**—One of the biggest reasons why your teen might be hesitant to open up to you is that they feel you'll be less-than-enthusiastic about their flaws and insecurities. They might also look up to you as someone who makes no mistakes and has everything figured out. Remember, only when you connect with your teen as the flawed human being you are can you help them be vulnerable and joyful with you. Let them know that not only is it expected for them to make mistakes but also that mistakes are key components in their journey of growth.

CONVERSATIONAL ROADBLOCKS

When we're trying to establish a connection with our teens, we might face some conversational roadblocks on our journey. Sometimes, for example, your teenager might not want to talk to you—no matter what you do. Other times, you might both be in a space where productive and healthy conversations are difficult to have. You could be fighting all the time, or you could have difficulty seeing each other's point of view. It's also possible that they or you are hesitant to say how you truly feel about a subject. For example, you might disapprove of someone in their friend circle, but you also don't want to alienate them by saying it out loud. How do you deal with these obstacles?

- **Take some time and plan your conversation with your teen:** If you feel like spontaneous conversations aren't helping you or your teen, prepare yourself for the conversation beforehand. Ask your teen when would be a good time to talk to them, especially if your conversations tend to get heated. You can also make a note of the points you would like to discuss with them during your conversation.
- **Reflect on your previous conversations:** What do you think you could have done better in your previous conversations with your teen? Were you too quick to judge them? Did you talk too much instead of listening to them? Did you allow your emotions to overwhelm you and the

conversation? I'm not saying that your teen couldn't have made mistakes. However, it's helpful to focus on the things *you* can improve during your conversations with them.

- **Ask them about the medium of communication they're most comfortable in:** This doesn't mean you should only communicate with them via text. Rather, your teen should know you're willing to connect with them at all costs. If your teen is not particularly keen on having a face-to-face conversation with you currently, let them know that you're open to talking through a medium that is comfortable for them. At the same time, express your interest in having a face-to-face conversation with them as soon as they feel ready.

- **Approach these conversations from a different lens:** If you go into a conversation wanting your teen to listen to you at all costs—or forcing them to see your point of view—that energy will permeate the entire conversation. Instead, why not think of your conversations as an opportunity for both of you to learn and grow together? Why not ask your teen to explain certain things that don't make sense to you? Why not see things from their perspective for a while? Your teen should feel like these conversations are more than a chance for you to question and invalidate their life choices.

EMPATHY AND VALIDATION

When we're communicating with our teens, we often clash with them due to the difference in our opinions and worldviews. Not only that, but our teens usually only feel responsible for themselves and their emotions —mainly because they are busy trying to make sense of this world. We, on the other hand, have a responsibility to protect our kids from the same world that they're intent on conquering. So—when we brush aside their emotions or dismiss their thoughts on certain issues— we're not doing it to hurt them but to protect them. We want our years of experience to count for something— to shelter them from heartbreaks and to make life a little easier for them. See, our intentions might be pure, but the effects our actions have on our teens aren't helpful at all.

An essential thing to understand is that by validating our teen's feelings, we're not necessarily agreeing with them. At the same time, we're telling them that their feelings are valid and that we see their pain and confusion. When we empathize with our kids, we show them that we love them and we're willing to see the world through their eyes. Here are a few things we can do to ensure we're validating our teen's experiences:

- **This is the time to put your active listening skills to use:** You need to give them your full attention and really listen to what they have to say. Don't interrupt them or ask too many questions when they're venting. Most importantly, reflect on what they're telling you. For instance, if they say they're upset, acknowledge their feelings and venture an educated guess as to why they're upset. Even if you're wrong, your teen will likely correct you once they feel validated by you.
- **Be mindful of the nonverbal cues you're giving to your teen:** Sometimes, we might not say it in as many words, but our gestures tell our teens that we don't take their feelings seriously. In many cases, we might not even realize that we've sent our teens those signals. For example, you might hear about a fight they had with their best friend for the tenth time and inevitably roll your eyes. You might be doing this because deep down, you know that they're going to get over it pretty soon, but your teen might see it as you ridiculing their situation. So,

make sure your nonverbal cues are kind and encouraging at all times.

Apart from these tips, you can also make a list of common validating and invalidating statements. These are very useful when you're still trying to learn how to be more empathetic toward your teen. Some examples of validating statements or questions are:

- I understand that you feel upset, angry, or tired.
- I can see why you're feeling this way.
- I can imagine how difficult today must be for you.
- It seems like this experience has affected you very deeply.
- I want to understand more about how you're feeling.
- Let me know if I can do anything to help you through this.
- What do you need from me at this time?
- I am so glad you decided to share this with me.

Here are a few common invalidating statements or questions you might be using with your teen:

- I don't understand how you can have such an intense reaction to something like this.

- I faced worse problems than you when I was a teen, and I never behaved in this manner.
- How long are you going to be affected by what happened? When will you get over it?
- At least it isn't as bad as it could have been. Be thankful for that.
- Why is it so difficult for you to be happy or to move on?
- Aren't you grateful for everything I do for you? Why would you make life so difficult for me?
- This isn't even a real problem.

One thing we need to understand is that our teens are not growing up in the world that we did. Many things that didn't exist for us—like having our entire lives online—are significant elements of their lives. So, we are often not equipped to understand how their surroundings contribute to their emotional and mental health. Therefore, it's even more needful to validate how they feel and to gently ask for more information that can make it easier for us to help them.

DISCUSSING SENSITIVE TOPICS

Discussing sensitive topics with our teenagers can always be awkward. In recent times, however, the challenges have multiplied—mostly due to the amount of exposure our teens have to the real world. Through social media, they are now aware of—and vulnerable to —a lot more than many of us were as teens. This creates a unique paradox for us. On one hand, our teens might know a lot more about certain subjects than we would expect them to. On the other hand, they might not have access to trustworthy sources of information —or reliable advice—about these topics. So, we need to ensure that they're prepared for this world as much as possible. Some of the topics that you might need to discuss with them are academic or learning difficulties, keeping secrets from you, money management, consumption of harmful substances, sex and masturbation, sexual and gender identity, bullying and relational aggression, and political views.

You don't have to deal with these topics all the time. In fact, you can even ask your teen to let you know if they want to discuss something sensitive with you. This will only happen if your teen trusts you to provide them with a safe and non-judgmental space for their feelings. Here are a few guidelines you can use if you're anxious about having these conversations with your teen:

- **Embrace the awkwardness:** There's no way around this. These conversations are going to be difficult and awkward. In many cases, your teen (and you) might be visibly embarrassed while discussing these issues. Understand that this is normal and that these discussions are necessary. You can only get over the awkwardness by getting used to these discussions.

- **Check-in with your teen at all times:** If your teen is absolutely not interested in discussing something with you, let them know that you are there for them whenever they are ready. Also, pay attention to the topics that make them most uncomfortable. They might have some triggers or limiting beliefs around them that you need to address.

- **Have a general discussion around the culture they're growing up in and how it affects them:** If you don't want to have specific discussions all the time, ask them questions about how their mental and emotional health is affected by social media, peer and adult expectations, and their own impulses. Keep these questions open-ended and respectful so your teen does not feel targeted.

- **Have a discussion regarding choices and consequences:** If you tell your teen what they should and should not do, chances are, they're not going to listen to you. In fact, many of us can make certain topics more interesting and attractive for our teens simply by treating them as taboo. Instead, have an open conversation with them regarding the choices they make and the consequences of those choices. Try not to scare them or make it sound like they will be punished. Instead, treat them as adults and make them understand they would have to deal with the consequences of their actions in the future.

- **Talk to them about peer pressure and individuality:** Peer pressure is the toughest thing for any teen to navigate, even as they try to figure out their individual beliefs and goals. Many teens are more or less sure about the things they don't want to participate in, but they have trouble defending their choices in their peer groups. Therefore, they might need your help in being assertive and speaking up for themselves. They might also need to know that you have their back if they feel isolated by their friends for sticking to their beliefs.

- **Go for positive rather than negative examples:** When we want to protect our children, we can often use scare tactics to get them to conform. Even though our intentions are pure, our actions can cause more harm than good. We don't want our teens to avoid talking to us because we scare them. We want them to want to discuss these topics with us because we make them feel better about themselves. So, wherever possible, use positive rather than negative examples. For instance, instead of always telling them about how addiction ruins lives, you can tell them what a life free of addiction looks like. You can talk about the mental, physical, and emotional benefits of not having to depend on substances to get through life.

- **Pay attention to the underlying impulse rather than the actions:** Don't get me wrong—your teen's actions are important. At the same time, it's more crucial to understand *why* they're behaving in a certain way. For example, if your teen is behaving in a manner that is too sexual, is it because they're looking for validation from someone? If your teen is engaging in reckless behavior, is it because they're trying to overcome their social anxiety? If your teen has been hiding things from you, is it because they feel like they should be loyal to their friends? When you understand the reasons behind your teen's behavior, you're better equipped to teach them about healthier ways to deal with these impulses.

- **Shift the conversation from shame and guilt to joy:** Many of these topics are difficult to broach precisely because they're shrouded in shame and guilt. Even if your teen wants to confide in you, they might feel ashamed of doing so. It's your responsibility to make the discussion joyful and full of possibilities. Talk to them about what makes them happy and how they can bring more joy into their lives.

- **Explore the possibility of therapy if your teen needs it:** Sometimes, the issues that your teen faces might not be easy for you to solve on your own. No matter how supportive you are, you might simply not be equipped with the tools needed to help your child deal with their emotions and heal from certain wounds. If your child cannot open up to you—no matter how hard you try—or if you feel like you're way in over your head when it comes to certain sensitive topics, there's no harm in exploring therapy as an option. The thing to keep in mind is that a therapist does not replace your role in your teen's life but merely supplements it.

DIGITAL COMMUNICATION ETIQUETTE

Our teens live in a world where most of their communication occurs through digital media. Especially after
the COVID-19 pandemic, almost all communication
has a digital angle to it. All of us can benefit from
learning digital communication etiquette, but our teens
need more help than most. This is because their
method of communication with others might be
extremely informal and also heavy on jargon that only
their peers understand. Also, as teens are chronically
online, they might share a lot more of their lives on
social media than necessary or advisable.

There are some points you can keep in mind when it
comes to digital communication etiquette for teens:

- They already know this, but remind them that
  whatever they share online remains online in
  perpetuity. Ask them to keep this in mind
  before engaging in online communication.
- Help them learn **proper email and video call
  etiquette** so that they can communicate
  effectively with people they study or work with
  in the future.
- When it comes to social media use, discuss with
  them things like **frequency of use, time spent
  on each session, and the kind of content**

they're posting or exposing themselves to. It's easy to believe that their virtual lives will not have an impact on their "real" lives, but this is simply not true. Make sure they know that what is healthy in real life is also healthy on social media. For instance, bullying or slandering someone isn't harmless just because it's not physically happening to them.

- **Addiction to adult content** is, unfortunately, becoming a major cause of concern for parents of teenagers. While the urges that underlie such behavior are normal, the way they channel them can be extremely problematic. It's tricky to get your child to open up to you about such behavior, but assure them that all you want is for them to be happy and healthy in every way. Some teens might require therapy to overcome these and other addictions as well.

In this chapter, we've understood how to communicate effectively with our teens. In the next chapter, we'll discuss about emotional intelligence in teens.

3

THE POWER OF EMOTIONAL INTELLIGENCE

How many times have you found yourself feeling helpless as your teen undergoes yet another outburst? How many times have you wondered what is behind your teen's silence? If you feel overwhelmed and unsure of what to do in the face of the numerous emotional challenges your teen goes through at this time, you're not alone. Instead of feeling powerless as a parent, why not use this time to teach your kids the value of emotional intelligence? Why not help them acknowledge and understand their own feelings while also teaching them to be compassionate toward the people they interact with? In this chapter, we'll learn all about emotional intelligence in teens.

WHAT IS EMOTIONAL INTELLIGENCE?

Simply put, emotional intelligence helps us master our emotions and not let them overpower us. Our emotions are extremely powerful signals that tell us what we want and who we are. They help us understand ourselves and others better, provided we don't run away from what they're trying to tell us. Since our teens go through puberty, various life changes, and the pressure to make something of themselves—all at once, they usually have a difficult time making sense of their own emotions. Also—as per our previous discussion—there is a lag between the working of the decision-making center and the emotional center of a teen's brain. This means our teens feel a lot of emotions at once—often conflicting—but don't always feel equipped to handle or think through them.

Emotional intelligence helps them label their emotions and respect what they're feeling without letting those feelings dictate their behaviors. At the same time, it allows them to understand why others around them are acting in certain ways. It helps them resolve conflicts, improve their relationships with both peers and adults and manage their emotions in a healthy manner. Not only that, but emotional intelligence teaches our teens to think beyond themselves and offer empathy and compassion to others. An effective emotional intelligence toolkit contains skills like self-awareness, self-compassion, empathy and compassion for others, interpersonal and social skills, and motivation to create any changes required. Let's discuss how to help our teens build this toolkit for themselves.

BUILDING YOUR TEEN'S EMOTIONAL VOCABULARY

Before your teen learns to manage their emotions, they need to recognize and accept them. This can be trickier than we think. Even as adults, we can often mistake one emotion for another. Also, the more we repress our emotions, the more they get entangled with other emotions. For instance, if our teen gets angry a lot, it can be difficult for them to understand whether they're truly angry or if they're using anger as a way to mask their fear. It's also useful to understand that our teens are growing up in a world that often makes it difficult for them to express their emotions. Or, let me put it this way. Your teen might find that some emotions are more acceptable to express than others. For instance, they might be part of a group where it is okay to display aggression but not okay to show vulnerability. Or, they might have internalized the message that there is no place for their complex emotions in their lives.

As a parent, you can help your teen become more confident in owning their emotions—especially those that are otherwise difficult for them. The first thing we can do is ask them to label exactly what they're feeling at a given moment in time. This will not always be accurate, but ask them to do it anyway. Also, don't do this when they're feeling exceptionally angry or triggered, as it might backfire. Instead, wait for them to cool down a bit and then try to make sense of their emotions. Often, our teens can struggle to label their emotions but can check in with themselves and see how their bodies are responding to these emotions. For instance, your teen can recognize that their body stiffens when they are stressed or that their face gets too hot when they're angry. Some of these signals can be more subtle than others; therefore, it can take some time for your teen to recognize them. That's okay. Let them know that this is a process.

Another component of building their emotional vocabulary is helping your teen connect their behaviors with their emotions. Often, it might seem like they're "acting out" or behaving in an irrational manner—not only to us but also to themselves. Once they start connecting the dots, so to speak, they will be better equipped to understand how they usually express their emotions. For example, let them make note of how they react when they're stressed. Do they give in to addictive behaviors like binge eating or substance use? Do they withdraw from their social life? Do they get more irritated during these periods? Encourage them to be honest with themselves and not give in to guilt or shame when they think about their behaviors. When our teen feels ashamed, their ego steps in to protect them, which can prevent them from gaining the self-awareness they need. Avoiding guilt can be extremely challenging, but you can help by letting them know that their emotions are valid.

When your teen builds their emotional vocabulary, they become more aware of

- their emotions in real-time,
- the physical, mental, and physiological effects of their emotions, and
- their behaviors in response to these emotions.

LEARNING EMPATHY AND COMPASSION

Apart from learning emotional self-awareness, teens also need to become more mindful of other people's emotions. For this, they need to learn both empathy and compassion. Let's first understand the nuances of empathy and compassion. Empathy means "putting ourselves in someone else's shoes and walking a mile in them." In other words, empathy allows our teenagers to understand how others are feeling at any given moment. There are two main types of empathy—emotional and cognitive. Cognitive empathy is *thinking* about how others feel in certain situations. For example, if you've never given birth, it might be impossible for you to understand how someone feels during that process. At the same time, you can learn about their feelings through books, documentaries, and first-person stories. Emotional empathy, on the other hand, is about being able to *feel* how someone else feels during an experience. For example, if you've undergone bullying, it can be easy for you to empathize with someone undergoing a similar experience—as you can remember how it is to feel ostracized, alone, and scared.

Empathy is an extremely needed tool for our teens to possess, as it allows them to understand experiences that aren't their own. Your teen might already be more empathetic than others, which is a great thing, but it can come with its own challenges. Compassion goes a step further than empathy. See, empathy can help you feel for someone, but it might not necessarily compel you to take action on their behalf. In fact, if we pick up on everyone's emotions but cannot do anything about them, it can get pretty exhausting for us. Compassion helps us do something to help others and make them feel better about themselves. For example, if your teen notices that one of their classmates is struggling to adapt to their surroundings, they can empathize with them. If they decide to help them become more comfortable in their own skin and make new friends, then they're exercising compassion toward them.

Another reason why compassion can be more powerful than empathy is that it can sometimes be very difficult for your teen to exercise empathy—especially when they're overwhelmed with their own emotions. For example, if your teen is feeling angry at a peer for treating them unfairly (in their opinion), it's almost impossible for them to see their peer's point of view at the moment. Sometimes, empathy can feel like a huge ask—as if our teen needs to ignore their own emotions to make sense of others'. During these times, compassion can come to our rescue. Even if our teens don't understand what another person is going through—or don't want to—they can practice compassion toward them by tapping into their humanity. They can also practice compassion by asking themselves what the kindest thing they can do for others in the moment is. Sometimes, compassion means that they don't say something harsh to the other person. Other times, it means providing space for another person's emotions along with their own. The good news is that both empathy and compassion can be learned over time.

Here are a few things you can do to help your teen develop both empathy and compassion:

- Encourage your teens to **expose themselves to different cultures and life experiences** through movies, books, and social media.
- Ask them to seek out **opinions that are different from theirs** when they read or watch things—on social media or otherwise.
- Let them write a letter to someone who is a stranger but who makes their lives easier. This could be someone who cleans the street where your house is or someone who serves them lunch at school. Even a **small letter of gratitude** can help your teens think beyond themselves.
- If your teen is **highly sensitive** or more empathetic than most, you might need to work with them to cope with the surge of emotions they undergo every now and then. We'll learn about some of these coping mechanisms soon.
- Pay attention to what your teen is angry or upset about—especially those things that are not directly related to them. Instead of dismissing those feelings or asking them to get over them, ask them to come up with solutions. Let them think about the **smallest action they**

can take to make things better for someone else.

- **Give yourself grace too**. Sometimes, we forget how difficult the work of empathy and compassion can be. Your work as a parent can be doubly challenging—because you need to acknowledge your teen's feelings and also make space for the people they need to be compassionate toward. "Compassion fatigue" is very real, so ensure that both you and your teen indulge in self-care activities that help you connect with yourself. This can be something as simple as walking outdoors or cooking and sharing a meal together.

ANGER MANAGEMENT TECHNIQUES

When our teens display anger, many of us either respond in anger or helplessness. Some of us punish our teens for showing anger. Others believe that anger is a major aspect of adolescence. The thing is, our teens have different ways of showing anger, and their anger can be extremely helpful in understanding them better. In fact, in some cases, our teens might not even be openly displaying their anger—which can be dangerous for their mental and emotional health.

The first step is to understand how your teen deals with anger. For example, does your teen show their anger by directing it outward in the form of aggression? This can be destructive, but it is easier to recognize. In some cases, teens can suppress their anger or direct it inward —either because they're warned against displaying anger or because they feel like no one will understand it. In such cases, they tend to blame themselves for feeling this way and can also develop mood disorders along the way. When anger doesn't find an outlet, it can lead to self-criticism and shame—sometimes even resulting in self-harming tendencies and eating disorders. In fact, experts believe that anger directed inward can lead to something called "smiling depression." In this condition, your teen might seem happy, well-adjusted, and even successful on the outside while being angry and depressed on the inside ("5 Evidence-Based Anger Management Techniques for Teens," 2022). A third way of dealing with anger is through passive-aggressive behavior. This behavior occurs when teens don't want to show their anger in an obvious manner, but they still want the other person to understand that they're upset. This can take the form of "silent treatment" and mean or sarcastic comments.

An interesting point to note is that both inward anger and passive-aggressive anger are exhibited more by teen girls. This is mostly because, in many cultures, women are not allowed to display their anger openly in front of others. When we shame our teens for feeling or showing anger—irrespective of gender—we lose the opportunity to connect with our teens. This doesn't mean that aggressive displays of anger are okay. What it means is that we can focus on what their anger signifies and help them work through their issues in a healthy manner.

Here are a few tips that might help your teen manage their anger better:

- **Talk to them about ways to manage their anger in the moment**: When your teen is overwhelmed by anger, the most important thing is for them to manage their symptoms and not cross the line. For instance, they can figure out how their body is reacting in the moment and try to manage those symptoms. Like, when their body temperature increases, they can cool themselves down by running their wrists through water. Similarly, if they find themselves getting breathless with anger, they can take deep breaths and calm down.
- **Discuss acceptable and non-acceptable behaviors**: You want your teen to believe that anger is a valid emotion, but how they communicate their anger is equally obligatory.

For example, shutting down when they are angry is not useful in the long run, but taking a break for some time is perfectly alright. Similarly, expressing their displeasure to others is fine, but becoming aggressive or behaving in a destructive manner is not. When you talk about behaviors that are not acceptable, make sure you let them know that repressing their anger is not a solution.

- **Pay attention to their triggers and the thoughts that accompany them**: A simple journaling exercise can help your teen pinpoint their triggers. It can help them understand who or what causes them to act a certain way and whether they can do anything about these triggers. For example, if it's possible for them to maintain their distance from someone who keeps teasing them, they should look for ways to do that. If it's not possible to avoid a trigger, what is the best way for them to manage it? What are some healthy ways in which they can channel their anger during such moments? Can they go for a walk? Can they take the support of friends they trust? They don't need to ignore every provocation. In fact, they can work on responding in a healthy manner to those who trigger them. Being aware of their triggers can go a long way in helping them constructively manage their anger.

- **Teach them the value of a mindful pause**: Anger is often extremely destructive because it spurs us to act on our emotions without thinking. In teens, this behavior is aggravated because their emotional responses usually override their decision-making abilities. Therefore, we can teach them to consciously induce a pause between their triggers and their responses. For example, if they can simply take a couple of breaths before responding to an event or person that triggers them—they might respond in a healthier manner. Sometimes, even saying something as simple as—*I am really angry right now and not in a space to make the right decision. Let me give myself 10 minutes before I react*—can help your teen clear their head and become more mindful of their response.

- **Try to understand what's behind their anger**: Once they've calmed down, ask your teen to think about why they were angry. Sometimes, anger is a way to deal with fear. For example, if your teen is angry at you for not allowing them to go to a party, it's probably because they fear missing out on an opportunity to bond with their peers. Similarly, if your teen seems angry and ungrateful about the food you make for them—chances are—they're struggling with their own eating habits and body image. Shame, guilt, and self-criticism can also manifest in the form of anger, which is why you might need to help them dig deep and look beyond the obvious answers.

STRESS REDUCTION TECHNIQUES

Adolescence is a highly stressful time for our children for a variety of reasons. During this time, they have to deal with changes within themselves as well as in the world around them. For the first time, they have a say in the decisions they make about their lives—and they're both terrified and exhilarated because of it. For some, this time comes with soul-crushing expectations from parents, teachers, and society. Your teen might be constantly worried that they'll fail to measure up. Not only that, but this is when they start taking their friendships and romantic relationships seriously. This means that any problems they face in their peer groups or other relationships weigh heavily on them. Apart from these concerns, many teenagers also face bullying, abuse, hostile environments, the death of loved ones, financial challenges at home, and other difficult conditions that can lead to elevated stress levels. It's also important to understand that—if managed properly—stress doesn't always have to be a bad thing. After all, stress can also originate because your teen has set certain goals for themselves or because they want to improve their performance. Identify the reasons for their stress and to come up with coping mechanisms for the same.

Here are a few steps you can take to help your teenagers manage their stress:

- **Look out for the warning signs**: Since adolescence is such a busy time for both parents and their children, it can be difficult to recognize earlier symptoms of stress in your teen. What you need to look out for are changes in their behavior that persist for a period of time. For example, has your teen started losing their temper more frequently than usual? Have they started eating too much or too little compared to their previous eating habits? Have their sleeping patterns changed suddenly? In some cases, your teen might even show certain physical symptoms like falling ill more frequently than usual. It's perfectly okay for your teen to have an off day now and then, but if these changes begin to disrupt their lives in a significant manner, you might need to step in.

- **Help your teen set a self-care schedule for themselves**: When your teen is set on conquering the world, self-care is usually last on their mind. Therefore, help them in creating a schedule that is simple and effective. For example, ensuring that they get eight hours of device-free sleep every day is crucial. Similarly, make sure they're eating nutritious meals as much as possible and getting regular exercise during the day.

- **Ask your teen what helps relieve their stress**: Some of their ideas will not align with yours, so try to come to a happy compromise. For instance, if they want to spend all their time scrolling through social media websites or playing video games, ask them to spend some of that time outdoors. Engage in fun activities with them, and encourage them to spend some time doing nothing. If they're engaging in unhealthy behaviors, suggest healthier alternatives instead of shaming them.

- **Encourage them to share their concerns with you or someone else**: If your teen feels comfortable confiding in you, ask them to share any concerns they might have with you. If they prefer talking to a friend or another trusted adult, encourage them to do so. What's important is that they have a healthy outlet for their emotions. If you think your teen might benefit from talking to a therapist, ask them about it. Some teens might not be comfortable talking to someone else yet, which is when journaling can help. This journal can help them feel like they're talking to a trusted friend without having to feel vulnerable with someone else.

- **Help your teen develop their problem-solving abilities**: If your teen stays focused on the problems they're facing, they might become more stressed over time. Instead, help them focus on finding solutions to their problems using critical thinking skills. Of course, some problems might not have immediate solutions, but recognizing this is also a skill. Also, encourage them to make mistakes as they try to find solutions to their problems. This way, they'll be less scared of failing and come up with creative ways to deal with their issues.

- **Model healthy coping behaviors for your teen**: As social media becomes an essential part of our teen's life, it becomes difficult for us to regulate the various entities that have an influence on them. For instance, your teen might be following influencers who promote unhealthy eating behaviors or unrealistic body types. Or, your teen might be a part of a group where everyone is an overachiever, and there's no space for making mistakes and being vulnerable. There's only so much we can do about the interactions that our teens have in the outside world. What we can certainly do, however, is show them what it means to be a healthy and well-adjusted adult. By being vulnerable with them, admitting to your mistakes, and loving yourself—you're showing your teen that there are ways of finding acceptance and joy within themselves. You're also providing a powerful narrative that counters the narrative they're being sold by popular media.

BUILDING RESILIENCE

Resilience is the ability humans have to bounce back from difficult situations. When two people face similar hardships in their lives, they don't respond to it in the same manner. One of them might get crushed by the challenges they have to face, while another might use these challenges to become stronger. Of course, this comparison only holds true when other factors in their lives are more or less similar. As your teen prepares themselves for a challenging life ahead, they will need to build their resilience over time. A resilient teen will be able to make the most out of difficult situations and use them to develop their abilities.

There are many factors that go into building your teen's resilience. Here are a few things you can focus on:

- **Is your teen confident enough?** Does your teen have a healthy sense of self-worth and belief in their abilities? Do they truly believe that they have a lot to offer to the world?
- **Does your teen possess gratitude and grace?** Is your teen thankful for what they already have, mindful of their privileges, and graceful in the face of challenges?
- **Does your teen have a positive mindset?** Is your teen able to handle situations with humor and positivity most of the time? Do they have a fixed view of themselves and the world, or do they believe that they can learn from their mistakes and grow as human beings?
- **Does your teen have a strong character?** Is your teen aware of their core values? Do they believe they should act with integrity as much as possible, and are they willing to do what it takes to stand by their values? Not only that but does your teen have a strong sense of purpose

and a vision to make this world a little better than they found it?

- **Is your teen able to look beyond themselves?** The more we look for ways to help others, the more resilient we become. This is because we focus on making other people's lives better, and we also gain perspective in the process. Is your teen keen on helping others? Are they able to see multiple perspectives when discussing issues? Do they show compassion in their daily lives?

- **Does your teen have positive connections in their life?** Do they seem supported and nourished by the people in their life? Do they enjoy healthy social and interpersonal connections? Do they have positive role models who help them deal with problems in a healthy manner? Are they focused on building meaningful connections with their peers?

- **How does your teen cope with problems in their life?** Does your teen resort to unhealthy behaviors like drinking, smoking, or disordered eating when they're stressed or anxious? Or are they able to channel their emotions in a healthy manner?

- **Does your teen have a sense of accountability?** If your teen frequently blames the whole world for their problems, they might not be able to cope with difficulties in a healthy way. Ask yourself if they have a sense of accountability for their actions. Are they able to take responsibility for their part in the problems they're facing? Do they feel like they have control over what happens in their lives?

It takes time to build resilience, which is why you need to be patient with your teen when they're dealing with a challenging situation. Let them know you have their back, but also encourage them to figure out the best way to deal with the situation at hand.

Now that we've discussed how to teach emotional intelligence to our teens let's move on to the important topic of conflict resolution.

4

CONFLICT AND RESOLUTION

Once your child becomes a teenager, your home might begin to feel like a war zone. Even without realizing it, you have suddenly become your child's "enemy," and everything you do (or don't do) is now a trigger for them. While it might sometimes feel like your teen *wants* to fight with you all the time, the truth is slightly more nuanced than that. In this chapter, we'll talk about why conflicts really occur and what you can do as a parent to ensure that both your teen and you understand each other better.

COMMON PARENT-TEEN CONFLICTS

The first thing we need to understand is why conflicts between parents and teens happen in the first place.

Before we go into the specifics, it's vital to remember that conflicts are not only common but also necessary in relationships. This is because a conflict allows both parties to be honest about the issues they're having in the relationship and also gives them an opportunity to resolve the issues before the situation deteriorates any further. If handled properly, conflicts can actually bring people closer together by building trust and encouraging vulnerability. Seen from this lens, your teen's outbursts and confrontational behavior might not be purely destructive in nature.

Think of it this way: Your teen is at a stage where they want to assert their independence through their decisions. They also want acceptance from their peers, which can make it seem like they don't want your approval anymore. This issue isn't as black-or-white as we might think. Even though our teens trip over themselves trying to convince us that they don't need us, they want us to see them as "adults." They want us to acknowledge their maturity, responsibility, and autonomy.

You might be compelled to think they want this because they feel confident in their ability to take on the world. In fact, it's often the opposite—meaning they want you to show faith in them when they don't feel confident in themselves. Think carefully about the last few times you've been in conflict with your teenager. Think about what they've said and why they've said it. Pay attention to the triggers, and dive deeper into why your teen reacted the way they did. For example, the last time your teenager asked you to go out with friends, and you refused, what were they angry about? On the surface, yes, they could have been angry about not being allowed to spend time with friends. It might also seem that their friends are way more needed to them than you are. At the same time, couldn't it also be that your teen is upset because they feel like you don't trust them? Could it be that they want to start making their own decisions, knowing they have your support— and when that doesn't happen, do they feel angry and helpless?

If we shift our perspective on why conflicts occur in the first place, we might be in a much better position to understand our teens' reactions. Here are a few common topics that can lead to frequent conflicts between you and your teen:

- **Curfew:** While your teen might love to stay out as long as they can, your priority is to ensure they are safe and well-rested at all times. Sometimes, you might even be concerned about the company they keep if they have a habit of coming home late.

- **Friendships and relationships:** You and your teen might clash over the friends they choose, whether or not they should engage in romantic relationships and the kinds of partners that are acceptable to both of you. Since their relationships have a huge impact on their mental and emotional health, it can be difficult to trust their choices all the time.
- **Appearance:** This is a period when your teen starts experimenting with who they are—which manifests in their appearance as well. They want to experience the latest fashions, change their hair, or accessorize themselves in ways that might be new or uncomfortable for you.
- **Communication:** Sometimes, we might have conflicts with our teens regarding differences in our communication styles. Other times, we might want our teens to be open and upfront with us at all times, while they might be wary about sharing certain aspects of their lives with us.
- **Digital devices and social media:** Your teen might find social media essential to their existence and growth, while you might be concerned about the effects of this exposure.
- **Their future:** Your teen is now at the threshold of adulthood, meaning they need to make

crucial decisions regarding the path they want to take in the future. This includes paying attention to their interests and abilities, as well as making practical decisions that serve them well materially and emotionally. Not surprisingly, a decision as important as this can cause a lot of conflict between you and your teen.

CONFLICT RESOLUTION STRATEGIES

It's normal to be wary of getting into conflicts with our teens—but if your teen is expressing displeasure regarding something, it means they are communicating with you. Let's not take that for granted. On that note, let's discuss some of the things we can do to resolve conflicts with our teens in a peaceful manner:

- **Keep your focus on the problem:** When we're overwhelmed by a problem, we often get frustrated at the person in front of us. Your teen is not the problem; instead, they're *facing* a problem in their lives. Work with them to find solutions, and don't end up alienating your teen because of your anger.
- **Pick your battles:** As parents, we often want to solve every problem in our teens' lives. That,

however, is next to impossible. Similarly, everything that you have an issue with might not be worth getting into an argument over. Carefully examine your reasons for pursuing a topic with your teen. For example, you might have issues with how they style their hair, but is that something you can let go of in favor of something more substantial—say, their career choices? This is also necessary because if you and your teen get into a conflict over everything, you'll be resolving nothing and wary of having honest conversations with each other.

- **Prioritize your teen's needs:** Even though you only want your teen to be happy and safe, your solutions might seem like "commands" to them. In order to convince your teen that you're always on their side, ask them about their needs. Listen to them carefully and empathetically, and choose a solution that works for both of you.

- **Trust your teens to make the right decisions:** It's okay to feel worried about your teen's ability to make the right choice for themselves, but you cannot start with distrust and hope that it leads to a healthy relationship between the two of you. Once you've communicated your expectations to them, you need to step back and trust that they will make the right decisions.

- **Focus on only one issue at a time:** When we get into an argument with our teen, we might feel like tackling all the problems at once—not least because it feels like a once-in-a-blue-moon chance to get through to them. However, not only does this take away focus from the issue at hand, but it also seems like you're trying to blame them for *everything* at once. So, unless two issues are really interconnected, try to focus on only one at a time.

- **Take accountability for your part in the conflict:** If you think that your teen is "responsible" for your conflicts, you'll never be able to resolve them in a healthy manner. After all, your teen will feel targeted all the time and will hesitate to communicate openly with you. Instead, let them know you're aware of your own shortcomings and show them that you're willing to overcome them for their sake.

SETTING BOUNDARIES AND DETERMINING CONSEQUENCES

An essential point of contention between parents and teens is the setting and maintenance of boundaries.

Setting boundaries can mean different things in different scenarios. For example, sometimes it means setting certain rules around your teen's schedule or activities. Other times, it means discussing the appropriate and inappropriate behaviors. In general, setting boundaries is all about respecting your teen's individuality and the need to experiment while ensuring their safety and proper development. It can be tricky to maintain a balance between healthy boundaries and too many restrictions when dealing with teens, so here are a few questions you can ask yourself:

- Which are the most imperative and urgent boundaries that you need to implement?
- Why are these boundaries important to you?
- How strict are these boundaries, and why?
- Which kind of boundaries are negotiable, and in what conditions?
- What are the consequences for your teen if they ignore or disrespect these boundaries?
- What is the best way to communicate these boundaries to your teen?

Here are some things to keep in mind while setting boundaries with your teens:

- **Build a healthy relationship with them first:** Setting boundaries can be tricky because they might make your teen feel like you're imposing your own "rules" on them. It gets trickier if your teen doesn't trust you or if they have trouble believing that you are on their side. So, spend as much as you can with your teen—bonding over your shared interests or taking an active interest in their life.

- **Focus on the positive behaviors you see or want to see in them:** Instead of talking about what they cannot do, focus on what they are already doing well or what they can do once the boundaries are in place. Tell them how these boundaries can make their lives better.

- **Model respect at all times:** What better way to show your teen the importance of respect than by being respectful to them at all times? Even if you're dealing with something difficult, be kind and understanding as much as possible. At the same time, it's your responsibility to stop your teen from crossing the line during conversations. Let them know that rudeness or bad behavior will not be allowed, no matter what.

- **Explain to them which boundaries can evolve over time:** For example, if your teen is younger, you might want them back at home by 9:00 p.m. As they grow older and demonstrate responsible behaviors, you can talk to them about extending their curfew. Also, let them know that some boundaries can be changed depending on the circumstances as well. For instance, if you're worried about your teen's safety—say, if there has been a sudden spurt in crime in your city—you can adjust their curfew till you feel that it's safe for them to stay out late.

- **Be clear and consistent around any boundaries you set:** When you've decided on and communicated a boundary to your teen, ensure that you honor it as much as possible. If you cannot do so for some reason, communicate clearly with your teen and let them know why you had to make an exception. Sometimes, these exceptions might even be in their favor. For example, you might typically not allow them to go to parties on school nights, but in a particular case, you might be very close to the parents, and they might assure you that they'll take care of your teen and bring them home within the curfew. Make them understand that the exception only reinforces the rule.

- **Talk to them about consequences:** Instead of focusing on punishments, explain to them the consequences of both maintaining and disrespecting boundaries. After all, boundaries are needed because your teen is trying to establish their independence. Let them understand that independence comes with a set of responsibilities. Clearly let them know what the consequences of their choices are, and follow through on them when the time comes. Your teen needs to know that they cannot take these boundaries lightly. In that vein, you need to ensure that these consequences are realistic for you as well. If you're unable to implement them, you're going to have a lot of difficulty making your teen take them seriously in the future.
- **Frame these boundaries as opportunities for taking on more responsibility:** Instead of dictating your terms to your teenager, you can ask them to make choices whenever possible,

provided they are able to bear the consequences of their choices.

- **Ask them about the boundaries you can honor as well:** This is a great way to build trust in your relationship and show your commitment to their independence. Ask them about the kind of (reasonable) boundaries that they would like you to maintain, and have an honest discussion about how these boundaries help them become mature and responsible adults.

HANDLING DEFIANCE AND REBELLION

While rebellion is a mainstay of adolescence, there are times when things get out of hand. It can be deeply unsettling when your teen acts defiantly almost all the time or when they seem to be at odds with you—no matter what you do. First of all, take a deep breath. Then, ask yourself the following questions to understand the situation better:

- What is your teen being defiant about and why?
- Is this an issue that has come up in the past, and has something been done about it?
- Is there a specific situation to blame for their behavior, or is something deeper at play here?

- How do you deal with your teen when they make mistakes or feel overwhelmed?
- How is your teen's current physical, mental, emotional, and hormonal health?
- Are there any specific triggers that cause your teen to lash out?

These questions will help you understand a few things, such as:

- If your teen is struggling with issues that aren't obvious to you—such as peer pressure, stress regarding their grades or future, or depression.
- If your behavior is causing them to act out in any way (This doesn't excuse their behavior, but it can help you recontextualize it more responsibly).
- If you can create an atmosphere at home that helps them regulate their emotions and openly communicate their problems with you.
- If your teen needs more attention from you or wants you to respect their opinion during discussions.
- If your teen needs professional help to manage their emotions in a healthier manner.

If your teen has been struggling with anxiety, depression, or similar mental health issues—and they're behaving rudely or being very difficult to communicate with in general—you should consider getting professional help. They might be suffering from oppositional defiant disorder.

CONSTRUCTIVE FEEDBACK: CRITICISM VERSUS PRAISE

As parents, we often think that our teens need to be praised every now and then, but not so much that they lose sight of reality. At the same time, we might underestimate how often we criticize our teens. This has been corroborated by some interesting research. A study asked parents to self-report the amount of praise and criticism they direct toward their children. At the same time, the researchers also observed their behaviors in a clinical setting. As it turned out, parents criticized their children almost three times as much as they praised them. This means they heavily underestimated how much they criticized their children, even as they correctly estimated how much they praised them (Swenson et al., 2016).

There are some things to keep in mind before you start feeling guilty about this behavior. Many of us might come from families where our parents were stingy with praise and generous with criticism. This doesn't necessarily mean they didn't love us; it was just easier for them to focus on our faults—in the hope that it could help us overcome those faults. In some cultures, it's less common for parents to lavish their children with attention because they feel it might spoil them. Also, some parents might want their children to "toughen up"— especially if they belong to marginalized communities. For example, my mom—who is the kindest, sweetest, and warmest mother I could hope for—has never been particularly effusive with praise. I used to get irritated at this, saying things like, "You never hesitate to criticize me, but you have a lot of trouble acknowledging my good qualities." In response, she told me that she already knew how amazing I was and that I should know how proud she was of me every day. It was necessary for her to criticize me so that I could become even more amazing by improving on certain aspects of myself. Her answer softened me up a bit, but it also made me realize that she never thought I might need some validation from her from time to time.

If you're someone who wants to create a healthy balance between praise and criticism, here are a few things you can do:

- **Pay attention to how you criticize your teen:** It's important for your teen to receive constructive feedback, but you should also be careful of how you convey your criticisms to them. Do you nag them often? Do you ignore their achievements and only focus on their drawbacks? Is your tone kind and respectful throughout the conversation? Do you criticize your teen or their behavior (there *is* a difference!).

- **Think about where your focus lies:** Are you focused on how your teen can improve with respect to their current self, or are you comparing them with their peers? Your teen should be able to understand that you're only focused on their growth and not on their trajectory with respect to others around them.

- **Examine your reasons for the criticism:** This is a critical one. Why do you need to criticize a particular action or thought of your teen? Is it because they're doing something that is harmful or wrong, or is it simply because you have a difference of opinion with them? If what they're thinking or doing is simply different from something you're used to, give it some time and try to understand their point of view as well.

- **Make sure you praise your teens in a genuine manner:** Your teens will be able to distinguish between genuine praise and insincere compliments. Resist the urge to give backhanded compliments as well, as it can mess with your teen's self-esteem. As parents, it is our job to model healthy behaviors for our teens, and offering genuine praise is an indispensable one.

- **Focus on the right thing to praise:** Often, we might focus exclusively on results. While it's important to recognize success and learn from failure, we can praise our teens for their efforts as well. In fact, encouraging them as they're trying to improve can ensure that they stay focused and hopeful on their journey—especially if they're trying to master something that isn't easy.
- **Your praise should be as detailed as possible:** Sometimes, we might offer generic praise to your teens, which might make them feel like you don't value them. You might also come across as distracted or uninterested. Instead, pay attention to what you want to praise about your teen's behavior. For example, instead of simply complimenting them on their project by saying,, "Good job!" or something like that, you can talk about the aspects of their work that stood out to you. So, you could say, "This is an extremely

creative way of discussing the subject. Kudos
to you!"

When it comes to both praise and criticism, it's a good
idea to ask for feedback from your teen. Talk to them
about what sticks with them and what doesn't, or what
makes them feel good and what lowers their morale.
You might not like everything they tell you, but as long
as they are respectful, their feedback can help *you*
provide more effective feedback to them.

THE ART OF FORGIVENESS

Adolescence is a time of intense emotions, which makes
it difficult for our teens to let go of hurt, anger, or
resentment toward the people they are in conflict with
—including their friends and parents. As uncomfortable as conflicts are, they come with opportunities for
us to teach our teens the value of forgiveness in their
lives. Not only that, but they can also help us brush up
our own forgiveness skills. Here are a few ways in
which we can practice the art of forgiveness with our
teens:

- **Explain to them the benefits of forgiveness:**
  The most common misconception about
  forgiveness is that it benefits the other party

and not us. Another one is that forgiving someone is the equivalent of excusing their bad behavior or forgetting their injustices toward us or others. This is simply not true. Explain to your teens how forgiving people makes them feel better about themselves, relieves any tension or stress they might be carrying within themselves, and helps them move on in their lives. It's better for their mental, emotional, and in some cases, physical health. One impactful way of getting our teens to understand the positive impact of forgiveness on others is to make them realize how they would feel if they made a mistake. Ask them how they would like to be treated by someone who is angry at them. Would they want the other person to try and understand their point of view? Would they like to be given a second chance? Would they like to be treated with respect even when the other person is angry or disappointed with them? Now, ask them if they can extend that same courtesy and grace to others when they're angry with them.

- **Don't force them to forgive people:** If you force or shame your teen into forgiving someone—they won't be sincere in their apology, nor will they understand why forgiveness is important to them. An insincere apology can sometimes seem worse than silence, so explain to your teen the importance of a meaningful and heartfelt apology. Also, give them some time so that they can be ready to forgive those who have hurt them.

- **Teach them that forgiveness doesn't mean overlooking unfairness:** This works on two levels. First, your teen should understand that they don't have to overlook bad behavior, such as bullying and harassment, just to forgive someone. They might need to take a stand against such behavior and even involve adults wherever necessary. There's a fine line between forgiving someone and being a pushover, and your teen can benefit from knowing the difference. Second, it's also essential for your teens to understand that if they cross certain lines, they will have to earn your forgiveness by proving that they're going to improve their behavior in the future. Some things are hard to come back from—even if you love someone a lot—and this is a vital lesson for your teens to remember. This way, they'll get better at setting and maintaining boundaries in the relationships they form in the future.

- **Help them understand that forgiveness is not transactional:** This point might seem like a contradiction of the last point, but it's not. In some cases, forgiveness is only possible if the other party actively tries to mend their ways. This is because their behavior has directly hurt us, and we're trying to protect ourselves from future pain. At the same time, forgiveness cannot be transactional. Meaning you cannot ask someone to do something for you in return for forgiveness. This is a lesson that we, as parents, might also have to keep coming back to.

- **Model forgiveness as a parent:** Do you struggle to forgive others in your life? Can you forgive your children or your partner without making it seem like you're doing them a favor? Are you frequently the person in a relationship who is rigid about not being the first one to apologize? Be careful about how you come across to your teens. A teen who sees their parent *always* get their way can learn to do the same in their relationships with others. A teen who sees forgiveness as a favor rather than as an act of grace will behave accordingly with others. If you can show your teens how forgiveness makes your life better, you'll have an easier time convincing them to do the same. This also means that your own apologies toward them or others shouldn't be defensive in tone or sound like an excuse. Take accountability in your own relationships, and you might be surprised when your teen begins to do the same in their life.

THE IMPORTANCE OF FAMILY MEETINGS IN CONFLICT RESOLUTION

Throughout the book, we've discussed the importance of staying in touch with your teens. One of the most effective ways of doing this is by scheduling regular family meetings. If, as a family, you're not used to sitting down and openly discussing your issues—this might be a great way to start. Also, family meetings don't need to be only about conflict resolution. These meetings give us a chance to connect with each other and to understand each other better. When we do this, we automatically reduce the chances of friction in our everyday lives. Your teen might understandably resist the idea of a family meeting, especially because it might seem to them like an opportunity for you to scold or correct them. It's your responsibility to explain to your teen that this family meeting is about connection and not conflict. One of the ways of doing this is by including fun games in the session or by asking your teen to talk about the things that they enjoy at school or at home.

In the beginning, you can start by scheduling a meeting once a month—so that your teen gets accustomed to the idea of it. Also, make sure that you don't schedule the meeting when they are stressed (for example, when they have an upcoming exam) or when you're preoccupied with something else. Being present throughout the meeting is imperative for everyone in the family. It's also useful to have a rough agenda in mind before you start the meeting so that you don't forget to discuss important things during the meeting. In the beginning, you can set the agenda of these meetings, but after your teen gets used to them, you can ask them to take the lead in planning them. This way, they will feel invested in the process and also gain a sense of accountability over time.

Your meetings don't need to be full of rules, but it's a good idea to lay out some guidelines that can keep your discussions on track. Over time, these meetings can not only help anticipate future conflicts and resolve current ones, but they can also teach your teens certain communication skills. For example, your teens might practice their reflective listening skills and also begin to appreciate perspectives that are different from theirs.

They can also learn how to assert themselves and talk about their needs healthily and respectfully.

Now that we've discussed healthy ways of resolving conflicts with our teens let's move on to fostering independence in our teens.

5

FOSTERING INDEPENDENCE AND AUTONOMY

Whether we like it or not, our teens demand independence from us during this phase of their lives. This brings considerable anxiety and apprehension in our minds regarding their safety and success. As worried as we might be about letting our teens experience the world on their own terms, we also have a responsibility to prepare them for it before they are hit with the demands of adulthood. The good news is that, with a little practice, we can teach our kids to balance their need for independence with a sense of responsibility that will serve them well as teens and adults.

BALANCING FREEDOM WITH RESPONSIBILITY

In an ideal world, parents would give their teens autonomy only when they were completely sure of their ability to handle the responsibilities that came with it. In the real world, our teens usually overestimate their ability to handle responsibilities, while we frequently underestimate them. It also doesn't help that the world is changing at a rapid pace, and what seemed like a niche skill a few years back is today considered an essential life skill. Therefore, parents are often confused about when to give their kids the freedoms they desire.

As scary as it might seem, giving our kids autonomy comes with a lot of advantages:

- It can make our teens proud of the decisions they make and also encourage them to take more initiative in their personal and academic lives.
- It can help them take more accountability in their lives, thus thinking about ways to learn from setbacks rather than finding people to blame for their problems.

- It might make them think about the values they stand for and the sacrifices they are willing to make to stay true to their beliefs.
- It can also be a great way of helping our teens understand how the world works and how it affects people of different cultures, backgrounds, and life stages.
- It might feel like a teen asking for autonomy is only thinking about themselves, but autonomy also gives them the opportunity to think about others. In fact, it's a powerful way of helping them understand how interdependent we are as humans.
- The ability to make their own decisions also comes with the responsibility of handling the consequences of those decisions.

If, as a parent, you're worried about which freedoms to give to your teen, think about it this way. Your teen only deserves those freedoms that they are capable of handling, which means they need to demonstrate a certain level of responsibility before they are given those freedoms. So, think about the times when your teen has shown maturity in their behavior or when they've shown responsibility in certain areas of their life.

During this time, you might be tempted to step in and make decisions for your teens every now and then. I would advise you to resist the urge unless your teen is in danger. Instead of calling the shots on every aspect of your teen's life, why not step back and assume the role of a trusted consultant? Why not offer your help and guidance to your teen when they need it and follow their journey as a proud parent at other times? Trust me, this is not an easy journey for any parent to make, but the pride that comes with seeing your teen take on the world far outweighs any trepidation you might experience in the beginning.

ENCOURAGING YOUR TEENS TO MAKE GOOD DECISIONS

The ability to make good decisions is a crucial part of your teen's "independence" journey. Another aspect is owning and learning from their bad decisions. How can you help them improve their decision-making skills at this time? The first thing you can do is help them determine the needed elements of good decision-making, such as

- setting goals for themselves,
- identifying why the decision is important to them,

- analyzing the pros and cons of each decision,
- thinking about how their decision affects others,
- taking the necessary steps required to see their decision through,
- reflecting on the decision and its consequences, and
- learning from any mistakes made in the process.

The next thing to do is to start giving them the autonomy to make decisions every now and then. Start with something small and relatively low-stakes, like creating their own schedule for a week—knowing that they don't have any major exams or events coming up that week. Let them decide how they want to spend their time and also clarify the consequences associated with each decision. After that, you need to step back and let your teen figure out how to manage their decisions and their consequences. After the week is over, you can sit down with them and talk about the highs and lows of their journey—the challenges they faced, the lessons they learned, and the confidence they gained in the process. Once your teenager begins to understand the responsibilities that come with decision-making, you can help them make bigger and more important decisions.

GOAL SETTING AND TIME MANAGEMENT

At this stage in their life, your teen will likely set goals for their future selves. Some of these goals will be academic and professional in nature, while others will be their personal life. No matter what their goals are, they'll need a proper plan and schedule to pursue them successfully. Also, your teen might struggle to manage their time well, not least because they have so much to do in such little time. They can feel overwhelmed with all the decisions that need to be made and might even give in to inertia and procrastination if they cannot manage their time anxiety.

If your teenager struggles with time management, spend some time with them explaining how managing their time can help in various ways:

- It can improve their academic and extra-curricular performance at school.
- It can help them think through their decisions and reflect on them.
- It might prevent any anxiety around major events, as your teen will be able to plan for these events in an effective manner.
- Time management helps your teens become more productive over time.

- It can free up time to pursue activities they enjoy and spend time with their loved ones.

Here are a few tips that can help your teen on their time management journey:

- **Help your teen identify the most productive periods of their day:** Of course, they'll still have to stick to their schedule regarding school, sports, or other activities—but they can use this knowledge to complete their projects or prepare for mandatory tests during their most productive periods.
- **Talk to them about SMART goals:** Teach them to set specific, measurable, actionable, realistic, and time-bound goals wherever possible. This way, they'll not only be able to track their progress over time, but they'll also be able to streamline their efforts toward achieving these goals.
- **Discuss the importance of prioritization and scheduling of tasks**: Often, teens struggle with understanding which tasks are obligatory and which are not. They might also have difficulty understanding the urgency associated with different tasks. Help them create a priority list of all the tasks they need to do. For example,

they might have a significant project due by the end of the month, which means they need to plan for that project in advance so that they don't have to scramble for time in the end. At the same time, they need to clean up their room as soon as possible, or they will have difficulty finding anything they really need. Some tasks will be urgent and essential, while others will be neither. Knowing the difference between these kinds of tasks is crucial for your teen, as is the ability to allow them the right amount of time.

- **Discuss how they can break larger tasks into smaller ones:** If your teen feels overwhelmed by tasks that seem intimidating in terms of the time and effort required to complete them, help them break these tasks into more manageable portions.

- **Teach your teen basic organizational skills:** So many teens struggle with time management because of poor organization skills. They waste a lot of time trying to figure out where something is kept—either in their rooms or on their devices. Teach them to create specific spaces for various important things in their lives and keep each thing where it belongs. This can be extremely challenging in the beginning, so help them track the amount of time it takes them to find things with and without organization. Also, help them make the organization as simple as possible.

- **Focus on the things that "eat up" their time and prepare for them beforehand:** It helps to remember that our teens might take more time to prepare for certain things than others. For example, they might spend a lot of time picking out the best outfit for school, or they might have difficulty ending their video game sessions in favor of studies. It helps to prepare for these situations beforehand. For example, even something as simple as picking out their outfit the night before school can help save a lot of time the morning after.

- **Shift from a "nagging" attitude to one of problem-solving:** When your teen seems to struggle with time management, you might get into a pattern of nagging them in the hopes of keeping them on schedule. However, doing this might alienate them from you and not even solve the main problems they're facing. For instance, if your teen has a habit of always procrastinating, why not work with them to understand why they do so? They might have perfectionist tendencies, or they might be dealing with severe anxiety about their studies.

Once you know what their challenges are, you can work with them to make the most of their time.

FINANCIAL LITERACY FOR TEENS

Adolescence is a period during which our children might start making spending, investing, and saving decisions independently for the first time. Not only that, but they might also start earning through part-time jobs, giving them more control over their finances. However, this doesn't necessarily mean they have the confidence and know-how required to manage their finances well. As parents, we can affect our teens' financial habits in a lot of ways. Here are some ways by which we can ensure that we have a positive influence on them:

- **Examine your own relationship with money:** Often, our teens learn their first financial lessons from us, even if we're not actively teaching them anything. For instance, if your teen sees you constantly worrying about money, they might develop an anxious relationship with money even if their financial condition is stable. Similarly, if your teen sees you hesitating to have open conversations regarding money, they'll have difficulty being transparent about their own financial concerns in the future. Make sure you model a healthy money relationship for your teens.

- **Teach them about the "time value of money":** As a teenager, one of the most powerful lessons your child can learn is related to the "time value of money." Simply put, this means that the earlier your teen starts investing their money, the greater the benefits of compounding that they can enjoy. So, even if they don't earn a lot or have a huge allowance right now, they can benefit a lot from investing this money wisely.

- **Emphasize the importance of having an emergency fund:** Before your teen starts saving and investing for the future, they should know how to protect themselves and their assets in case of emergencies. At this stage, they might not need an "emergency fund" as they have their parents looking out for them, but this is a valuable lesson that will help them immensely in the future.

- **Talk about debt before you give them a credit card:** Explain to your teen that certain kinds of debt can help them achieve some of their goals in life—for example, an education loan—but others can seriously come in the way of their financial and mental health, such as credit card debt. Since teens are usually influenced by their peers, they need to understand how credit card debts can wreck their lives. You can give them a credit card for a trial period and see how they fare before deciding whether they can be trusted with one.

- **Create a budget with them:** If you want your teen to handle money responsibly, the best way to go about it is by letting them create and stick to a budget for a week or even a month. You can help them create a simple budget that takes care of the basic necessities of the house as well as some of their own wants. Explain to them the difference between needs and wants and also about the responsibilities that come with discretionary spending. Once your teen creates their own budget, they might be able to re-examine their own demands and consider which ones are fair and which aren't.

- **Keep it simple and fun:** You don't need to burden your teen with tax receipts and overly complicated budgets right in the beginning. It can be a gradual and fun process for both of you. Even something as simple as going grocery shopping together—and comparing the prices of various items—can be an enlightening experience for your teen.

- **Talk to them about securing their assets:** This works on two levels. First, your teenager needs to understand the importance of insurance— especially health insurance—in protecting their future assets. Second, your teen needs to secure their assets online, especially as most of their transactions will be conducted virtually. This includes protecting their data and privacy, choosing authentic sites for transactions, and being aware of phishing attacks.

TEACHING LIFE SKILLS

When it comes to life skills, the sooner your teens start learning them, the better it is for their future. Life skills are those skills that help us live comfortably and safely in most cases. Your teen might be overly dependent on you for things like tidying up their room, doing their laundry, and cooking for them. While they don't need to be experts in all these areas right now, they do need to fend for themselves if you're not around. In fact, this is a great way of knowing whether your teen is ready to take on more responsibility in their lives. Start small, especially when it comes to chores that relate to the outside world. Let them know that you are there for them in case things go wrong, but give them the freedom to explore a little. Here are some of the life skills that you can focus on:

- Doing laundry, especially in terms of knowing how to separate the whites from colors, bedsheets and linens from woolens, and so on.
- Tidying up their room on a regular basis—including knowing how to use the vacuum cleaner and organizing all the items carefully in their room.
- Making their own bed in the morning and knowing how to fold clothes and bedsheets.
- Doing the dishes—with or without a dishwasher.
- Using all the necessary home appliances safely and efficiently.
- Doing basic maintenance work, like fixing a lightbulb or unclogging the sink. They should also know who to contact in case they need professional help at any time.
- Shopping for groceries for the entire family, keeping in mind any special dietary requirements of family members. Also, they should know how to read nutrition labels and determine if certain foods are fresh or not.

- Dressing up according to the weather and occasion at all times, and choosing clothes that are sustainable and value-for-money.
- Setting up appointments for themselves and others and being able to follow up with the concerned parties if needed.
- Driving, swimming, and other skills that might be important in the area where you live. You can choose to teach them these skills when you feel that they're ready for them.
- Cooking a simple and (as much as possible) nutritious meal for themselves while being safe in the kitchen.
- Being able to figure out the directions— especially without the help of online maps.
- Learning problem-solving skills—especially critical thinking and integrating feedback—and applying them in various areas of their lives.

PREPARING YOUR TEEN FOR THEIR CAREER

This is a crucial time for your teenager as they decide what they want to do for at least the next few years of their life. This can be a little scary for both you and them, but you should see it as an opportunity for your teen to explore their interests further. Here are a few tips that can help you and your teen during this vital phase of their lives:

- **Ask them to explore as much as they can:** Ask your teen to write down what interests them and why. Then, they can make a list of possible career paths where they can utilize these interests. They can also visit education fairs and talk to mentors—both at school and otherwise —in order to understand which career path might work best for them.
- **Encourage them to challenge themselves:** One of the best ways of doing this is by getting them to take up more challenging subjects— such as advanced placement courses—at school. This way, they might also surprise themselves with a passion they didn't even know they had.
- **Help them maintain a balance between their dreams and reality:** No parent cherishes this aspect of their job, but it is your duty to help your teen realize their dreams without losing sight of reality. Instead of dismissing them when they express an interest in a field that might not be very lucrative, ask them for a plan that might help them sustain themselves and stay true to themselves at the same time. Offer them a reality check, albeit gently, and ask them

NURTURING EFFECTIVE PARENT-TEEN COMMUNICAT... | 127

for a contingency plan if things don't go their way. This way, you can be in their corner while also encouraging them to take accountability for their choices.

- **Let them know that they don't have to decide everything today:** Sometimes, our teens might be pushed to think that they have to make all the right decisions today. You can help them realize that this is not true. Talk to them about the mistakes you've made along the way or when things haven't gone according to plan. Also, let them know how life has a way of working out as long as we stay in touch with our authentic selves. Your vulnerability can help take some pressure off them and let them know that no decision is fixed in stone.

Now that we've discussed how to foster independence and autonomy in our teens let's harness the power of cognitive behavioral therapy to support our teens.

6

COGNITIVE BEHAVIORAL STRATEGIES FOR FAMILIES

When we find our teens stuck in destructive patterns, we sometimes feel hopeless about their ability to get rid of these behaviors—and the thoughts and feelings that accompany them. What's more, we might also need help in dealing with our own limiting thoughts around our relationship with our teens. Cognitive behavioral therapy (CBT) is a great tool that the entire family can use to address negative thought patterns, emotions, and behaviors and to transform their family dynamics.

WHAT IS COGNITIVE BEHAVIORAL THERAPY?

Think about the last time your teen behaved irrationally or destructively. Maybe you gently pointed out a mistake of theirs, and they reacted extremely angrily. Or, they fought with their best friend and got upset like it was the end of the world. As a parent, you might be able to see that their behaviors are not in line with the challenges they're facing, but how do you make them see it too?

CBT is a tool that is a part of talk therapy, and it is commonly used to help people identify dysfunctional patterns of thinking, feeling, and behaving. It can also help us restructure negative thoughts, which can then affect our behavioral patterns. The concept underlying this process is that our thoughts give rise to emotions, which affect our behaviors. In fact, all three of them are interdependent on each other. Therefore, by managing our emotions and restructuring our thoughts, we can affect our behaviors as well.

There are many ways in which CBT can help your teen, such as:

- It can help your teen identify cognitive biases in their thinking patterns and also help them substitute their negative thoughts with more positive ones.
- It can help your teen overcome anxiety, depression, PTSD, phobias, substance abuse, and disordered eating behaviors.

- CBT can help your teen manage their emotions in a healthier way—especially when they're stressed—thus helping them overcome addictive behaviors.
- It can help improve their self-worth and self-esteem and become more compassionate toward themselves.

What makes CBT incredibly powerful as a tool is that it allows us to change our own thoughts and behaviors actively, thus giving us the ability to change our lives. Not only that, but these sessions usually come with many practical exercises, which are both engaging and empowering for teens. What's more, if your teen (and you) commit yourself to these exercises, you might see results quickly. For instance, on average, people need 15 CBT sessions to register an improvement in their mental and emotional health. Many different types of CBT sessions can help your teen, such as one-on-one sessions, parent-child therapy, and group CBT.

CBT TECHNIQUES FOR PARENTS AND TEENS

You can use these techniques for yourself, especially when you feel overwhelmed as a result of your teen's behaviors. You can also help your teen develop routines based on certain CBT techniques. Let's discuss a few of them in this section.

Cognitive Journaling

Cognitive journaling can help your teen engage in *metacognition*—in other words, they can now think deeply about their own thoughts and thinking mechanisms. They can also understand how their thoughts impact their behaviors in different scenarios. Each time your teen faces an unpleasant situation, they can— when they've calmed down—try to understand their own behaviors through journaling. For example, they can describe the situation in detail and also note how this situation affected them physically, mentally, and emotionally. Once they're aware of their emotions, they can note down the exact thoughts that passed through their mind at the time, as well as the behavior that they exhibited as a result.

The key lies in the details. The more detailed their description is, the more in-depth their analysis can be. It can be unpleasant to note down their negative thoughts and the consequences of their behaviors in detail, but it's an important step in understanding themselves better.

Cognitive Reframing or Reconstruction

Through the cognitive journaling exercise, your teen should be able to identify the emotions and thoughts they are experiencing at the time. When stressed, angry, or anxious, we often find ourselves stuck in a cycle of negative thoughts. Cognitive restructuring can help us reframe these thoughts in a more positive light without letting go of reality. In other words, we don't need to dismiss or ignore our feelings and thoughts completely. Instead, we can acknowledge our concerns without allowing cognitive distortions to overpower us.

Here are a few examples of cognitive distortions:

- **All-or-nothing thinking:** If your teen suffers from all-or-nothing thinking, they might see things and people either as "good" or "bad." In other words, they might not have any capacity for nuance in their lives. For example, if they have a disagreement with someone, they think that the person is "bad," "unreasonable," or "toxic." Sometimes, this can also mean they follow or praise someone unequivocally, thus placing them on a pedestal. This kind of thinking can prevent them from having meaningful relationships in their lives, and it can also make them experience higher highs

and lower lows during their interactions with
others.

- **Catastrophizing:** If your teen has a habit of
  catastrophizing, they will usually anticipate the
  worst possible outcome whenever something
  goes wrong. For instance, if they're in a fight
  with their best friend, they'll assume that their
  entire friendship is at risk or that their friend
  hates them. This can lead to extreme anxiety as
  well as destructive behaviors.
- **Fortune-telling:** Your teen might be in the
  habit of making assumptions and jumping to
  conclusions. For example, if they perform
  poorly on a test, they might say something like,
  "I'm really stupid and am never going to do well
  in life." You might wonder how one test can be
  the indicator of their entire life, but your teen is
  convinced about their fate.

When we reframe these negative thoughts, we first look
at the situation or trigger it through a neutral lens. This
means that if our teen has a fight with their best friend,
they will acknowledge this fact without attaching their
own opinion to it. After that, they will notice any
cognitive distortions in their thought process. For
example, they'll ask themselves why they assumed one
fight could end their friendship. Is it because they've

been having some other problems in their friendship? Has their friend become distant over time? Did their friend say or do something to indicate that they don't want to be friends with your teen anymore? Or, has your teen gone through a previous experience that has made them wary of friendships in general?

Once your teen understands the reasons behind their reaction, they can then reframe the thought they have into something more positive. For example, they can say to themselves *I feel sad and angry because of my fight with my friend, but that doesn't mean that our friendship is over. Once I feel calmer, I can reach out and try to sort things out with them.* Similarly, if they haven't done well on a test, they can say something like *I'm disappointed that I didn't do well on this test, but I now have an opportunity to learn from my mistakes and perform better on the next one.*

Problem-Solving Using Cognitive Behavioral Therapy

When our teens are preoccupied with negative thought patterns, it can be difficult for them to see beyond their immediate frustrations and look for solutions that might help them. A CBT-based approach to problem-solving can have a lot of benefits, such as:

- It gives your teen the ability to identify which problems can be solved and which cannot.

- It allows them to understand the time it can take to solve certain problems, helping them move on from a state of instant gratification.

- It can help them develop a systematic approach to solving their problems; this gives them the confidence to face their problems.

- When your teen knows what needs to be done, they'll be able to take effective action and not avoid their problems—especially through destructive behaviors.

- It helps your teen identify their stressors, barriers to progress, and support systems during times of crisis.

- A problem-solving approach helps your teen take a step back and not let their emotions overwhelm them.

- This approach also helps them gain perspective and look at their problems through various lenses, thus allowing for the formation of creative solutions.

Here's how you can help your teen get used to a problem-solving approach when dealing with issues in their life:

- **This is a great opportunity for you to practice "guided discovery" with your teen:** This method allows your teen to come to the required solutions themselves, albeit with the help of the questions you pose to them. You can ask your teen a certain set of questions that will help them clearly define their problem—which is extremely important for problem-solving— and understand the triggers that led to this problem. The answer to each question will lay the foundation for the next. For instance, if your teen seems really irritated lately, you can ask them questions about their day or week and help them understand what is triggering their irritation.

- **Help your teen set SMART goals in order to make a decision:** Once your teen identifies and defines their problem, they need to first make sure that this problem is solvable—at least in parts. For instance, if the cause of their irritation is a new member of their academic group—who they don't get along with—they cannot avoid them. Therefore, the solution has to enable them to maintain a cordial work relationship with them without getting ruffled in the process. Sometimes, the goal could be related to a change in behavior, while other times, it could simply be about gaining acceptance in their own lives.

- **Help your teen come up with alternatives and choose a viable one:** Often, our teens find themselves stuck in negative thought patterns because they cannot find a way out of their problem. This might also be why they resort to addictive behaviors in some cases. Therefore, helping them see that they have a few alternatives can also ease their mental load. Of course, each alternative comes with its own set of consequences, and your teen should be aware of them as well.

- **Help your teen evaluate their decision and learn from it:** The last aspect of problem-solving is often the most important. Without adequate feedback, your teen might not understand why a certain approach worked for them, which means that they might repeat the same problematic behaviors when faced with a similar problem next time. Therefore, they must become aware of the pros and cons of this decision and learn their lessons from it.

MANAGING ANXIETY AND DEPRESSION IN TEENS

Adolescence can be such a trying time for our teens that it might be difficult for us to differentiate between normal teenage angst—and the pains of growing up—and mental health issues like anxiety and depression. Of course, no one other than a licensed medical professional can diagnose these conditions with accuracy. At the same time, you should know when your kids are struggling with anxiety and depression so that you can get them the help they need and also provide solutions at home.

Here are a few symptoms you need to look out for:

- **Your teen is constantly sad, angry, or irritable:** Here, it's important to note that your teen will likely experience these emotions every once in a while, but if they seem to have settled into these moods, there might be cause for concern. Also, your teen might exhibit signs of depression in ways that are different from the norm. This means they might not seem sad or upset to you, but they might become furious at the slightest provocation. Look out for a marked change in your teen's behavior.

- **They might be experimenting with harmful substances:** When your teen is anxious or depressed, they might give in to peer pressure and experiment with drugs and alcohol to provide temporary relief to themselves. Of course, these substances only exacerbate their problems in the long run.

- **They have started engaging in reckless behavior:** For instance, your teen might engage in reckless driving, violent behaviors, and unsafe sexual behaviors. Apart from being dangerous, these are also signs that your teen might be trying to "feel something" by tapping into the adrenaline rush these behaviors produce.

- **Their lifestyle has taken a turn for the worse:** This can include their sleep routines, eating habits, exercise regimen, and even their hygiene habits. If your teen has trouble getting out of bed or showering (more than usual), or if they've made some drastic changes to their diet, it could be a sign that they're struggling with mental health issues. Also, a change in eating habits—coupled with signs of low self-esteem— could be an indicator of eating disorders, which are linked to both anxiety and depression.

- **They are dealing with self-esteem issues:**
  While it's normal for your teen to doubt
  themselves every now and then, it can be
  concerning if this becomes a pattern. If your
  teen is always feeling guilty or blaming
  themselves for everything that goes wrong in
  their lives—they might be trapped in a cycle of
  negative emotions. Also, if your teen becomes
  overly sensitive to criticism, they might be
  dealing with anxiety or depression.

- **Their performance has gone down at school:**
  If your teen has been struggling to perform well
  at school for quite some time—and this was not
  the case before—they might be dealing with
  mental health issues. Not only at school, but
  your teen might also lose interest in the
  activities they usually enjoy. Of course, your
  teen's interests might simply have changed, or
  they might have concerns about their career
  path—but it's a good idea to check in with them
  at this time.

Many of these symptoms might be short-lived and
related to hormonal imbalances or simply the stresses
that come with being a teenager in today's world.
Therefore, pay attention to how long these symptoms
last, as well as how severe they are. In the end, you

know your teen best, so you are best suited to know when they need professional help.

Once you identify the concerning symptoms in your teens, what can you do to help them manage their condition? There are some situations where you need urgent professional intervention—for example: If your teen begins to exhibit suicidal tendencies or even mentions suicide in a casual manner. In other cases, you might still need professional therapy and medication while at the same time providing your teens with the support they need at this time.

An important thing to keep in mind is that there are many reasons that can contribute to your teen's mental health issues. While genes and brain chemistry can certainly be at play, your teen's familial and social environment, relationships with their peers, and social media usage can also be extremely influential factors. What this means is that you can help your teen improve their mental health by helping them deal with these issues.

Here are a few ways in which you can provide support to your teen:

- **Show your teen that you're always listening to them and are always available for them:** If your teen is depressed, they might not be in a place to share their concerns with you in the beginning. This is where a professional therapist can help. At the same time, your teen needs to know that they have you in their corner whenever they need support. So, let them know that you're willing to listen to them whenever they are ready. Sometimes, you might have to be a little persistent to show your teen that you care about them.

- **Respect your teen's feelings and experiences:** When we see our teens struggling with their mental health, all we want to do is rid them of their pain. Sometimes, this can lead to us dismissing what might seem like trivial issues to us but are significant problems to them. It doesn't matter if you think that something is not worth getting anxious or depressed over. You should acknowledge the impact it is having on your teen's mental and emotional health. Over time, your teen should be able to see for themselves what is real and what isn't.

- **Check-in regularly with your teen:** As we discussed earlier, your teen might be anxious or depressed because of certain challenges in their life. For instance, your teen might be dealing with bullies at school or online, questioning their own identity, or experiencing loneliness in their lives. Knowing what their issues are might take time, but they will help you implement a problem-solving approach to your teen's issues wherever possible.

- **Understand the impact of social media on your teen's mental health:** The connection between social media use and teen health is complex. When our teens are anxious or depressed, they might start spending more time on social media for two reasons. One, it could act as a distraction for them. Two, it could give them more reasons to stay trapped in their negative thought processes. The reverse is also true. This means excessive social media use can also lead to anxiety and depression—or exacerbate their symptoms—by trapping your teens in an endless cycle of comparison, external validation, and distorted thinking. An interesting aspect of social media that sometimes gets ignored is that, in some cases, social media can actually improve your teen's mental health. Hear me out. If your teen is struggling with loneliness or with questions regarding their identity, social media might come to their rescue. For example, if you belong to a marginalized community and your teen doesn't have enough support from people around them, they can become a part of online groups that make them feel welcome. Of course, social media use and virtual groups should not take the place of offline interactions, but they can certainly make your teen feel less alone in some cases. As their parent, it's your job to appreciate these nuances and monitor their social media use accordingly.

- **Help them stick to a healthy lifestyle as much as possible:** Understand that when your teen is dealing with mental health issues, they might not always be able to care for themselves. Therefore, you might have to meet them halfway in some aspects. For example, you can create a healthy eating schedule for them but allow certain treats every now and then. Or, you can ask them to go for a walk every day, but also let them play video games on some days. Show them that you're not trying to force discipline on them but that you're trying to

work out a regimen that works for them during
this time.

- **Be patient with them at all times:** During this
time, you might have to strike a balance
between being gentle and being firm with your
teen. You might also need to understand that
you cannot wait for your teen's mental health to
improve for them to follow certain habits. For
example, your teen might insist that they can
only exercise when they feel better about
themselves. On some days, you can agree to
this. On others, however, you might need to
show them that even 15 minutes of gentle
exercise can improve their mood. The same
goes for their diet. If they're able to reduce their
dependence on ultra-processed foods, they
might actually experience an improvement in
their mood. Whatever you do, be patient with
them throughout this process. Remind yourself
that your teen isn't trying to make life difficult
for you or deliberately sabotaging themselves.
In fact, they want to get well as soon as
possible; it might just take them a while to get
there.

- **Take care of your mental health as well:** This
can be extremely easy to overlook. Taking care
of a teen who is dealing with mental health

issues can take a toll on our own mental and emotional health, not least because it can make us feel like an inadequate parent. Therefore, it's imperative to find support from other parents, professionals (if needed), and in self-care activities like daily journaling. This is where the various CBT techniques discussed earlier can come to your rescue.

Now that we've discussed how CBT can help us master our emotions, thoughts, and behaviors as a family—let's learn about mindful parenting techniques in the next chapter.

7

MINDFUL PARENTING FOR EMOTIONAL MASTERY

P arenting a teen can seem like a battle on a good day, which is why you might feel constantly over-whelmed and tired as a parent. The same goes for your teen. On any given day, they're trying to figure out their lives while also trying to honor their truth. Also, they might not show it, but they're conscious of your expec-tations of them as well. When you combine all of this, it's no wonder that your relationship is almost always laced with worry, anxiety, and guilt.

In this chapter, we'll learn all about mindful parenting in the hopes that both you and your teen can enjoy your bond in the present—without getting too caught up in the past or the future. What does it mean to be a mindful parent? To understand this, we need to under-stand what mindfulness is. Mindfulness is more than a practice. It's a state of mind where we can fully embrace the joys and challenges of the present moment without getting stuck in our feelings and thoughts. You might find this an impossible task, especially because it feels like it's your job to worry and your teenager's job to cause worry. However, with a little practice, both you and your teen can reap the benefits of mindfulness in your lives.

MINDFULNESS TECHNIQUES FOR TEENS

While these techniques can help your teen regulate their emotions and reduce stress, they're equally useful for you. In fact, a great way of getting your teen interested in a consistent mindfulness-based practice is by doing these exercises with them.

Using the Power of Their Breath

If your teen does not have the time to dedicate to meditation—or if they're unsure about its efficacy—ask them to simply focus on their breath when they're worried or upset. When they focus on their breathing, it acts as a grounding exercise for them—causing them to slow down and reflect on their feelings and thoughts. At the same time, the physical act of inhaling and exhaling deeply can help in stress reduction. When they feel triggered, ask them to pause and take three deep breaths before focusing on the problem at hand. They can also try paced breathing or box breathing to prolong the calming effects of the exercise. In paced breathing, they need to exhale for a longer time than they inhale. For example, if they inhale for five counts, they need to exhale for seven or eight counts. When they do this, their heart rate will decrease slightly, thus helping them relax.

Box breathing is about creating a "box" with your breathing patterns. For instance, if you inhale for four counts, you need to hold your breath for four, exhale for four, and then hold again for another four counts. This way, you can not only induce your body into a state of deep relaxation, but you can also improve the quality of your sleep. One thing to keep in mind during these exercises is that you should focus entirely on your breath and not get stuck in negative thought patterns. Of course, these thoughts will enter your mind during these exercises, but you don't need to dwell on them. Acknowledge these thoughts and emotions and gently bring back your focus to your breaths.

Getting in Touch With Their Body

The simple act of getting in touch with the sensations that our body experiences during stress or anxiety can help in overcoming these emotions. For this, your teen needs to close their eyes and focus on their body for at least 10-15 minutes each day. As they inhale, they need to focus on a certain part of their body and assess how they feel. For instance, they can focus on their stomach and note that it feels knotted up. This can indicate that they're under extreme stress and need to relax. Once they've acknowledged this sensation, they can exhale deeply and let go of the stress that has accumulated in their body. This is known as conducting a body scan. Once they become confident in this technique, they can conduct quick scans on their bodies whenever they feel overwhelmed.

Another exercise they can do to relieve tension in their body is known as "progressive muscle relaxation." In this exercise, they simply need to target one muscle group at a time, for example, their arms, legs, or shoulders. They can conduct a body scan to figure out which areas need the maximum attention, or they can do these exercises by engaging their whole body. During this exercise, they need to create tension in a particular muscular group and then release it suddenly (but without hurting themselves). Throughout the exercise, they need to keep breathing gently and steadily. This alternate tension and relaxation can help relieve stress and anxiety.

PRACTICING MINDFULNESS AS A PARENT

What are some things you can do as a parent to make your teen feel supported and understood? Here are a few tips that can help you:

- **Practice curiosity, openness, and non-judgment as much as you can:** One of the most important tenets of mindfulness is the absence of judgment. This is hard to practice because judgment is often combined with genuine concern for your teen's safety. However, I've found that nothing trumps judgment like curiosity. When you have a conversation with your teen and don't understand something, don't be quick to dismiss it. Instead, ask the questions that can help you understand. In general, be curious without being nosy when it comes to your teen's life. Your teen will notice when you ask them questions only to censure their choices. Therefore, make sure that your questions come from a place of openness to learn more about your teen as they learn more about themselves.
- **Always practice a mindset of acceptance:** This doesn't mean that you have to agree with everything your teen chooses for themselves.

What it means is that you need to understand your teen's journey, even if it isn't what you have in mind for them. When our teen chooses a path that seems alien to us, it can feel like they're rejecting us, but this is not true. In fact, no one is more scared than your teen about having to make all these important choices and face their consequences. So, they need to know that their parents will be there for them if things don't go according to plan. If you simply cannot accept the choices they make, let them know what your concerns are, and assure them that you're still on their side—even if you're struggling to understand their point of view. Your teen might appreciate your honesty more than you think.

- **Maintain the sanctity of your relationship with your teen:** Often, when we're frustrated or worried, we might ridicule our teen's choices in front of other parents. This can create a bond between the two of you but also undermines your relationship with your teen. Of course, you can talk about your struggles with other parents to feel supported by them, but you don't need to push your teen under the bus for that. Keep your concerns generic as much as possible, and never reveal anything that your teen has told you in confidence. While you won't do this intentionally, we can all get carried away when we're at our wits' end. If you need help with certain issues, try talking to a professional.

- **Don't weaponize your teen's vulnerabilities against them:** When we're in a fight with our teen, we might sometimes say things that can cause a lot of hurt. Remember to keep your boundaries in mind even when you're angry. Most importantly, make your teen feel safe by respecting their vulnerabilities. If your teen is sensitive about something, or if they've shared their insecurities with you—don't throw them back in their face when you're angry with them. The hurt caused by these actions goes beyond the fight or disagreement and might even cause them to distrust you in the future. Let your teen know that you're going to protect them at all times—even from your own anger.

CULTIVATING GRATITUDE AS A FAMILY

One of the most deceptively simple ways of becoming more mindful is by practicing gratitude as a family. Gratitude is related to mindfulness in an amazing way. When we count our blessings, we focus on all the things that we have in our lives right now. This way, our focus shifts from the regrets of our past and the apprehensions regarding our future. It also helps give meaning and depth to the present moment.

Both you and your teen can spend some time in the morning and at night going over the things and people you're thankful for. You can even exchange messages of gratitude with each other—reminding yourselves that you have a lot to be thankful for, even when things are challenging. Don't pass up an opportunity to thank your teen for all that they do for you. Similarly, make sure your teen understands that they are protected and taken care of by a lot of people.

Model gratitude for your teen by being thankful to everyone who makes your life easier. Appreciate your partner as much as you can, thank your parents for all their help and support if they're still around, and extend your gratitude toward cleaners, mailmen, and other service workers in your life. Show your teen that none of us can survive without the help and kindness of others.

If possible, ask your teen to write a letter of thanks to those people and circumstances that have made them stronger in the long run. Those experiences might not have been pleasant, but they would have helped your teen become stronger and wiser. This isn't something that can be done when their anger or hurt is still fresh in their mind, but they can surely appreciate these lessons when they feel less triggered and upset. This simple exercise can help them reframe challenges in a positive manner and free themselves from the endless cycle of guilt and blame.

Now that we've discussed how to master mindful parenting, let's end the book with a discussion on building a lasting connection with our teens.

8

BUILDING LASTING CONNECTIONS

Once you've established a healthy connection with your teen, you would like to strengthen this bond over time. Both you and your teen will evolve as human beings over the years, and so will your bond with each other. What are some ways in which you can embrace change while ensuring that you stay close with your child? We'll discuss a few of these methods in this chapter.

CREATING MEANINGFUL FAMILY TRADITIONS

Depending on your cultural background—and your communal and familial relationships—you might already have many traditions you celebrate as a family.

However, as your teens grow up, they might not feel attached to all these traditions. Here are a few ways in which you can maintain your connection with your teen over various family traditions:

- **Don't go overboard when it comes to traditions:** While not having enough traditions can lead to distance between you and your teen, too many of them can dilute the significance of these traditions for your family. Your teen should find these traditions significant enough for them to participate wholeheartedly in them. Similarly, your traditions don't have to be elaborate all the time. Even a few simple rituals can make these traditions meaningful for you and your teen.

- **Choose traditions that resonate with both of you:** This also means that you might have to let go of certain traditions that don't carry the same weight for you or your teen as they did earlier. If need be, create new traditions that excite both of you and keep evaluating these traditions from time to time. Remember, a tradition needs to evolve with you, not hold you or your teen back.

- **Stay flexible regarding certain aspects of the tradition:** As your teen grows up, they'll be busy forming new relationships and new traditions. During this time, it might sometimes feel like they aren't prioritizing your relationship with you, but that's not the case. In fact, you can use this time as an opportunity to tweak certain aspects of your beloved traditions so that they can still participate in it. For instance, if you both enjoy spending your birthdays together—but cannot manage for one year—think of ways to connect with them virtually and be present with each other during that day.

- **Pay attention to your teen's interests:** If you and your teen have spent a lot of holidays baking together, it might upset you that they aren't interested in baking anymore. Instead of seeing this as a rejection on their part, ask them what they would like to do from now on. Maybe they would like to go to a pottery class with you or treat you to dinner. Be open to these changes because it means that your teen is trying to stay connected with you.
- **Find ways to spend quality time with your teens whenever you can:** As your teens become busier in their lives, it is possible that you might not be able to keep up with your traditions. In that case, try to spend quality time

with them whenever you can. Don't get hung up on the details or even on the length of time you have with them. Instead, focus on making every moment count. Try not to nag your teen or discuss tricky topics with them when you're trying to enjoy yourselves.

MANAGING SIBLING RELATIONSHIPS

Sibling relationships are intricate enough that they deserve a book of their own. In this section, we'll simply touch on certain things you can do to ensure that your teen has a harmonious relationship with their sibling for the most part:

- **Don't compare your children with each other:** As obvious as this piece of advice is, we can often forget it when we're stressed or irritated. If you have more than one teen, you have your work cut out for you. If one of your children is considerably older than the other, you can expect them to be responsible for their younger sibling in some way. However, make sure that you don't make your teen feel inadequate in any way.
- **Make sure you protect your teen's individuality at all times:** Your children don't

have to be clones of each other to be successful and well-adjusted individuals. Saying things like "Why can't you be more like your brother?" or "I never had this problem with your sister" will only undermine your teen's confidence and make them feel like a misfit among their own family members. So, treat every child as a unique individual and help them figure out their life on their own terms.

- **As much as possible, let your children resolve their differences on their own:** Siblings have a way of resolving their differences on their own over time. Their conflicts can also be a great way to help them understand each other. Therefore, you don't need to step between them unless things get very serious. Of course, make sure that they don't cross any boundaries—such as engaging in physical violence or disrespecting each other.

- **Help your younger child navigate any feelings of confusion or loneliness:** If your teen is the elder one among your kids, your younger child might suddenly feel alienated from their elder sibling. The same sibling, who was once a constant source of support and an always-available playmate, might not be interested in spending time with them anymore. They might also seem more irritable or preoccupied than before, which can be confusing for your younger child. During this time, you need to be extra attentive toward your younger child and even act as a bridge between both your kids every now and then.

PREPARING FOR THE EMPTY NEST

After having spent years of our lives ensuring that our teens grow up into well-adjusted adults, it can feel strange when they are finally ready to leave their homes behind. As a parent, you'll likely experience a whole range of emotions—from pride at your teen's progress to anxiety regarding their safety and well-being and from excitement for their journey ahead to grief over the end of an era. There are many variables that determine how acutely we feel this grief over our teen's departure. For instance, if you're a single parent, you're likely to have a very strong bond with your teen— which means that the grief you experience might be much deeper. Similarly, if your teen is an only child, you might have greater difficulty recovering from their departure.

NURTURING EFFECTIVE PARENT-TEEN COMMUNICAT... | 165

At the same time, it's not all doom and gloom. There
are benefits to becoming an empty nester, such as

- **It can give both you and your teen a chance to
  evaluate your relationship from a distance:** If
  you frequently clash with each other, this is an
  opportunity to appreciate each other's absence.
  Even if you enjoy each other's company, a little
  distance can help you appreciate each other
  even more. A little breathing space can do
  wonders for any relationship.
- **It can give you an opportunity to re-evaluate
  your own identity:** If you've spent all your life
  being a parent to your teen, you might have
  difficulty seeing yourself through any other
  lens. However, once you spend more time with
  yourself, you might get an opportunity to
  discover facets of yourself that you had no idea
  about. You could be talented at something
  you've never tried before, or you could be great
  at helping others in your community. If nothing
  else, you might discover that you enjoy your
  own company much more than previously
  thought.
- **It can help you give time and attention to
  other relationships in your life:** Being a
  parent can often be a demanding full-time job,

which leaves little energy or time for nurturing other relationships in your life—especially if your teen needs extra care or attention. Once your teen is ready to move through this world as an adult, you can start building new relationships in your community, as well as nurturing your old ones. For instance, this can be a great opportunity for you and your partner to get closer to each other and strengthen your relationship.

Here are a few tips that can help you stay prepared for the "empty nest syndrome":

- Talk to your teen about how you'll stay in touch with them, including the frequency and intensity of your interactions.
- Discuss certain methods by which you can stay updated about their situation even when they're busy. This can especially help when you have anxiety about their safety.
- You can also come up with ways to contact each other in case of an emergency so that neither of you feels neglected when you really need the other person.
- Try to create a new schedule for yourself— filling up your extra time with certain activities.

You can start with group activities, just so that you stay accountable and also feel less lonely in the beginning.

- Carve out some much-needed me-time. You might feel like all the time you have is yours, but it's not as simple as that. When we're missing our kids or grieving the loss of their constant presence in our home, we might not even be aware of time passing by. Therefore, dedicate some time that you can spend on self-care activities.

- Look for ways to connect with others— volunteer in your community, schedule date nights with your partner, and build connections with both friends and strangers.

- Give yourself some time to grieve. It's unrealistic to expect that you'll be okay as soon as your teen leaves home. You're going to grieve for some time before you can appreciate the possibilities of this new phase in your relationship. Don't rush this process, as it's a testament to your enduring love for your teen.

- Check-in with your teen as well. Many parents assume that their teen is more than happy having "escaped" home, but this doesn't mean they don't miss you. In fact, they'll likely have some trouble adjusting to a new environment, and they'll appreciate you being there for them when they need you.

In the end, remember that doing a good job as a parent means that our children don't need us to navigate their lives anymore, but they would love to have us around anyway. What is a greater cause of celebration than that?

CONCLUSION

Parenting a teen can be such a roller-coaster ride that we often forget to enjoy the ride before it's over. What's more, our intention to protect and nurture our teens during this phase of their lives can be what keeps us from becoming their friend and confidante during this tumultuous journey. When it comes to parenting, hindsight is often 20/20. It's also true that no one has perfected the art of parenting till now, and maybe that's the point. Maybe parenting your teen isn't so much about perfection as it's about vulnerability. Maybe it isn't about fear and worry as it's about exploration and joy. This book was written to make parents like you have faith in the journey and to revisit your relationship with your teen. Here are a few things that we've learned from this book:

- In the first chapter, we discussed all about the teenage brain, in an effort to better understand the challenges they face during this time. We also discussed how your teen's environment can affect their physical, mental, and emotional development.

- The second chapter was all about creating a safe and effective space for communicating with your teen. We talked about the importance of both verbal and nonverbal communication, active listening, empathy, and validation in gaining our teen's trust.

- The third chapter was dedicated to building emotional intelligence in your teens. We talked about building our teen's emotional vocabulary, helping them become resilient and compassionate, and teaching them anger management techniques.

- In the fourth chapter, we dealt with the important topic of conflict resolution. We learned about the common reasons for such conflicts, as well as the most effective strategies for conflict resolution. We discussed the importance of setting and maintaining boundaries with our teens, handling rebellion, and offering constructive praise and criticism when needed. Last but not least, we discussed the importance of apologizing and forgiving during conflicts.

- The fifth chapter helped us foster a balance between independence and responsibility in our teens. We discussed goal-setting, financial literacy, building life skills, and helping them prepare for a career in the future.
- The sixth chapter helped us understand how to use cognitive behavioral therapy as a family to help our teen overcome negative thought patterns, anxiety, depression, and addictive behaviors. These strategies can also be used by us to overcome our own emotional and behavioral challenges as parents.
- In the seventh chapter, we discussed the advantages of mindful parenting and also discussed how we can practice mindfulness along with our teens. We also talked about using gratitude to create a deeper relationship with our teens.
- In the last chapter, we talked about the importance of creating traditions as a family to strengthen our bond with our teens. We also talked about the importance of managing sibling relationships, especially as they evolve over time. Last but not least, we discussed the effects of "empty nest syndrome," including the

benefits of having an empty nest. We also talked about ways in which we can make the most of this period of our lives.

I hope that this book gives you the confidence to work on your relationship with your teen and also helps you gain faith in the future of your connection.

Also, if this book has helped you in any way, I request you to leave a review on Amazon so that others might pick it up and be inspired by it.

REFERENCES

Abblett, M. (2019, June 13). *A mindfulness practice for stressed-out parents*. Mindful. https://www.mindful.org/when-parenting-gets-tough/

Active listening. (n.d.). Centers for Disease Control and Prevention. https://www.cdc.gov/parents/essentials/toddlersandpreschoolers/communication/activelistening.html

Anxiety and how to manage it: pre-teens and teenagers. (2022, October 19). Raising Children Network. https://raisingchildren.net.au/pre-teens/mental-health-physical-health/stress-anxiety-depression/anxiety

Apter, T. (2009, January 19). Teens and parents in conflict. *Psychology Today.* https://www.psychologyto

day.com/us/blog/domestic-intelligence/200901/teens-and-parents-in-conflict?amp

Balancing freedom and boundaries without going out of your mind. (2016, May 31). Parenthetical. https://parentheti cal.wisc.edu/2016/05/31/balancing-freedom-and-boundaries/

Beck, C. (2021, October 12). *5 fun ways to support emotional vocabulary.* The OT Toolbox. https://www.theottoolbox.com/5-fun-ways-to-support-emotional-vocabulary/

Betts, J. (2023, May 3). *Common problems between parents and teenagers.* LoveToKnow. https://www.lovetoknow.com/parenting/teens/parent-teenager-problems

Breehl, L. (2023, March 27). *Physiology, puberty.* Stat-Pearls - NCBI Bookshelf. https://www.ncbi.nlm.nih.gov/books/NBK534827/

Brower, T. (2021, January 3). *Gratitude is good: why it's important and how to cultivate it.* Forbes. https://www.forbes.com/sites/tracybrower/2021/01/03/gratitude-is-good-why-its-important-and-how-to-cultivate-it/

Building resilience in children and teens. (2023, January 3). Newport Academy. https://www.newportacademy.com/resources/well-being/resilience-in-teens/

Capecchi, S. (2022, June 8). *Mindfulness for teens: How it works, benefits, & 11 exercises to try.* Choosing Therapy. https://www.choosingtherapy.com/mindfulness-for-teens/

Characteristics of emotional development in adolescence. (n.d.). Article1000.com. https://article1000.com/characteristics-emotional-development-adolescence/

Cognitive development. (n.d.). HHS Office of Population Affairs. https://opa.hhs.gov/adolescent-health/adolescent-development-explained/cognitive-development

Cognitive development in adolescence. (n.d.). University of Rochester Medical Center. https://www.urmc.rochester.edu/encyclopedia/content.aspx?ContentTypeID=90&ContentID=P01594

College and career readiness: 5 ways to prep your students . (2022, September 7). Renton Prep. https://rentonprep.org/college-and-career-readiness-5-ways-to-prep-your-students/

The common sense census: Media use by tweens and teens, 2021. (2022, March 9). Common Sense Media. https://www.commonsensemedia.org/research/the-common-sense-census-media-use-by-tweens-and-teens-2021

Compassion vs empathy: what is the difference? (2021, November 2). tonyrobbins.com. https://www.tonyrob bins.com/mind-meaning/compassion-vs-empathy/

Conflict management with pre-teens and teenagers. (2021, September 8). Raising Children Network. https://rais ingchildren.net.au/teens/communicating-relation ships/communicating/conflict-management-with-teens

Creating meaningful family traditions. (2020, January 14). Forever Families. https://foreverfamilies.byu.edu/creat ing-meaningful-family-traditions

Cuncic, A. (2023a, February 13). *How to stop negative thoughts.* Verywell Mind. https://www.verywellmind. com/how-to-change-negative-thinking-3024843

Cuncic, A. (2023b, November 20). *What is problem-solving therapy?* Verywell Mind. https://www.verywell mind.com/an-overview-of-problem-solving-therapy-4767991

D'Amico, P. (2017, February 28). *5 ways to strengthen a parent-teen relationship.* Paradigm Treatment. https:// paradigmtreatment.com/strengthen-parent-teen-relationship/

Deupree, S. (2023, August 11). *CBT for kids & teens: How it works, examples, & effectiveness.* Choosing Therapy. https://www.choosingtherapy.com/cbt-kids-teens/

Difficult conversations with pre-teens and teenagers. (2021, September 8). Raising Children Network. https://rais ingchildren.net.au/teens/communicating-relation ships/tough-topics/difficult-conversations-with-teens

Driscoll, L. (2023, November 4). *10 simple activities to build a feelings vocabulary.* Social Emotional Workshop. https://www.socialemotionalworkshop.com/feelings-vocabulary-activities/

Eames, C. (n.d.). *Get parenting tips.* Texas Department of Family and Protective Services. https://www.getparent ingtips.com/tweens-and-teens/discipline/setting-boundaries-for-teen-behavior/default.asp

Eberly, S. (2012, May 18). *Learning digital etiquette—Tips to help teenagers.* Your Teen Magazine. https://yourteen mag.com/technology/teenagers-technology-manners

The effects of teenage hormones on adolescent emotions. (2022, September 30). Newport Academy. https:// www.newportacademy.com/resources/empowering-teens/teenage-hormones-and-sexuality/

11 habits for cultivating gratitude. (2023, April 20). a Little Dose of Happy. https://aldohappy.com/cultivating-gratitude

11 tips for communicating with your teen. (n.d.). UNICEF Parenting. https://www.unicef.org/parenting/child-care/11-tips-communicating-your-teen

Emotional development. (n.d.). HHS Office of Population Affairs. https://opa.hhs.gov/adolescent-health/adolescent-development-explained/emotional-development

Emotional development. (2016, December 1). Encyclopedia Britannica. https://www.britannica.com/science/emotional-development/Adolescence

Family meetings for family functioning. (2018, November 14). Spokane Christian Counseling. https://spokanechristiancounseling.com/articles/family-meetings-for-family-functioning

50 thought-provoking questions to ask your teen. (2020, July 15). Youth First. https://youthfirstinc.org/50-thought-provoking-questions-to-ask-your-teen/

5 evidence-based anger management techniques for teens. (2022, September 18). Newport Academy. https://www.newportacademy.com/resources/empowering-teens/anger-management-techniques/

Flannery, B. (2023, July 20). *Causes of conflict between parents and teenagers*. WeHaveKids. https://wehavekids. com/parenting/Sources-of-Conflict-Between-Parents-and-Teenagers

Fraser-Thill, R. (2022, November 2). *27 family traditions to enjoy together*. Verywell Family. https://www.verywell family.com/family-rituals-meaning-examples-3288187

Gehl, M. (2018, June 6). *Mindfulness for parents*. ZERO TO THREE. https://www.zerotothree.org/resource/ mindfulness-for-parents/

Ginsburg, K. (2022, August 4). *Cognitive development: thinking on new levels*. Center for Parent and Teen Communication. https://parentandteen.com/adoles cent-cognitive-development/

Gongala, S. (2023a, November 6). *21 essential life skills for teens to learn*. MomJunction. https://www.momjunc tion.com/articles/everyday-life-skills-your-teen-should-learn_0081859/

Gongala, S. (2023b, November 13). *Teen rebellion: Why do they rebel and how to deal with it?* MomJunction. https://www.momjunction.com/articles/teen-rebellion_00389300/

Griffin, A. (2017). Adolescent Neurological Develop-ment and Implications for Health and Well-Being.

Healthcare, 5(4), 62. https://doi.org/10.3390/healthcare5040062

Harpaz, B. J. (2009, September 8). *Teach teens life skills: Laundry, budgeting.* Today. https://www.today.com/today/amp/wbna32735738

Harris, D. (2020, February). *Heart to Heart – Conversations & connections that matter.* Augusta Family Magazine. https://www.augustafamily.com/heart-to-heart-conversations-connections-that-matter/

Hernandez, B. (2021, March 6). *7 tips for teaching mindfulness to Teens.* The Mindfulness Meditation Institute. https://mindfulnessmeditationinstitute.org/2021/03/06/7-tips-for-teaching-mindfulness-to-teens/

Hoose, N. A.-V. (n.d.). *Peer relationships | Adolescent psychology.* Lumen Learning. https://courses.lumenlearning.com/adolescent/chapter/peer-relationships/

Hougaard, R. (2020, July 8). *Four reasons why compassion is better for humanity than empathy.* Forbes. https://www.forbes.com/sites/rasmushougaard/2020/07/08/four-reasons-why-compassion-is-better-for-humanity-than-empathy/?sh=791d00e7d6f9

Houston, E. H. (2019, June 17). *CBT for children: A guide for helping kids in therapy.* PositivePsychology.com.

https://positivepsychology.com/cbt-for-children/
#issues

How to cope with stress: Stress relief strategies for the whole family. (2020, November 15). Bright Horizons. https://www.brighthorizons.com/resources/Article/coping-with-stress-and-stress-relief-strategies-for-the-family

How to deal with a rebellious teen. (2022, February 14). Newport Academy. https://www.newportacademy.com/resources/restoring-families/rebellious-teen/

How to help children and teens manage their stress. (2019, October 24). American Psychological Association. https://www.apa.org/topics/children/stress

How to help teenagers make good decisions. (2022, December 8). Spark Their Future. https://www.sparktheirfuture.qld.edu.au/how-to-help-your-teen-make-good-decisions-about-school-and-life/

How to help teens when they make bad choices. (2022, December 8). Spark Their Future. https://www.sparktheirfuture.qld.edu.au/why-teens-make-bad-choices-and-how-you-can-help-them/

How to practice gratitude. (2023, December 1). Mindful. https://www.mindful.org/an-introduction-to-mindful-gratitude/

How to talk to your teens about sensitive topics. (2013, November 1). *Stop Medicine Abuse.* https://stopmedicine abuse.org/blog/details/how-to-talk-to-your-teens-about-sensitive-topics/

Introduction to CBT. (n.d.). Cognitive Behavioral Therapy Los Angeles. https://cogbtherapy.com/intro duction-to-cbt

Iraheta, N. (2022, July 28). *How to validate your teen's feelings.* Health and Healing Therapy. https://www.healthandhealingtherapy.com/how-to-validate-your-teens-feelings/

Jain, P. (2022, October 14). Importance of financial literacy for teens. *Times of India Blog.* https://time sofindia.indiatimes.com/blogs/voices/importance-of-financial-literacy-for-teens/

Jennifer. (2022). *Identifying and managing your emotions.* The Center for Growth. https://www.thecenterfor growth.com/tips/addiction-recovery-identifying-and-managing-your-emotions

Jewell, T. (2020, November 16). *How to talk to your teen about sensitive topics.* Neighborhood Outreach Access to Health. https://noahhelps.org/how-to-talk-to-your-teen-about-sensitive-topics/

Jiménze, J. (2021, July 16). Compassion vs. empathy: Understanding the difference. *BetterUp*. https://www. betterup.com/blog/compassion-vs-empathy? hs_amp=true

Kaur, M. (2023, March 13). *How to resolve conflicts with your teen*. Shri Harini Media Ltd. https://www.parent circle.com/how-to-resolve-conflicts-between-parent-and-teenager/article

Keiling, H. (2023). What is emotional intelligence? Definition, key elements and examples. Indeed.com. https://www.indeed.com/career-advice/career-devel opment/emotional-intelligence

Kendra Cherry. (2023a, May 2). *Emotional intelligence: How we perceive, evaluate, express, and control emotions*. Verywell Mind. https://www.verywellmind.com/what-is-emotional-intelligence-2795423

Kendra Cherry. (2023b, June 5). *Compassion vs. empathy: What's the difference?* Verywell Mind. https://www.very wellmind.com/compassion-vs-empathy-what-s-the-difference-7494906

Kennedy, I. (n.d.). *Get parenting tips*. GetParentingTips.-com. https://www.getparentingtips.com/kids/relation ships/sibling-rivalry-in-children-and-teens/default.asp

Kenny, U., O'Malley-Keighran, M., Molcho, M., & Kelly, C. (2016). Peer influences on adolescent body image: friends or foes? *Journal of Adolescent Research, 32*(6), 768–799. https://doi.org/10.1177/0743558416665478

King, C. (2022). 30 curated positive parenting quotes that will inspire you to be a better parent. *Mama Instincts®*. https://mamainstincts.com/positive-parenting-quotes/

Kinsey, B. (2023, October 18). The happy teen: A delicate balance of freedom and responsibility. *Ensemble Therapy*. https://www.ensembletherapy.com/blog-posts/the-happy-teen

Klein, Y. (2023, June 21). Six ways you can validate a teen (and anyone else!). *Evolve*. https://evolvetreatment.com/blog/six-ways-validate-teens/

Klynn, B. (2021, June 22). Emotional regulation: Skills, exercises, and strategies. *BetterUp*. https://www.betterup.com/blog/emotional-regulation-skills?hs_amp=true

Langley, M. (2012, December 18). *Pregnancy, parenting, lifestyle, beauty: Tips & advice*. Mom.com. https://mom.com/kids/5098-nonverbal-communication-teenagers

LaScala, M. (2021, November 2). *The best empty nest advice for parents whose kids are leaving the coop*. Good

Housekeeping. https://www.goodhousekeeping.com/life/parenting/a38834/empty-nest-advice/

Lautieri, A. (2019a, March 18). *Resilience: Identifying and managing emotion.* MentalHelp.net. https://www.mentalhelp.net/emotional-resilience/resilience-identifying-and-managing-emotion/

Lautieri, A. (2019b, March 21). *Balancing praise and criticism.* MentalHelp.net. https://www.mentalhelp.net/self-esteem/balancing-praise-and-criticism/

Learning how to discipline your teen: Balancing freedom and structure. (2020, October 23). *Solstice East.* https://solsticeeast.com/blog/learning-how-to-discipline-your-teen-balancing-freedom-and-structure/

Li, P. (2023, September 16). *10 tips on how to deal with a rebellious teenager.* Parenting for Brain. https://www.parentingforbrain.com/rebellious-teenager/

Makvana, H. (2023, November 23). *10 important conflict resolution skills for teenagers.* MomJunction. https://www.momjunction.com/articles/important-conflict-resolution-skills-for-teenagers_00106119/

Managing screen time and digital technology use: Strategies for teenagers. (2022, October 28). Raising Children Network. https://raisingchildren.net.au/teens/enter

tainment-technology/screen-time-healthy-screen-use/managing-screen-time-teens

Mathew, H. S. (2023, May 25). *10 netiquette rules your teen must observe to be respectful and keep safe on the internet.* Shri Harini Media Ltd. https://www.parentcircle.com/internet-etiquette-rules-for-teens/article

McBurney, L. (n.d.). *A strategy for resolving parent-teen conflict.* Focus on the Family Canada. https://www.focusonthefamily.ca/content/a-strategy-for-resolving-parent-teen-conflict

McNutt, M. (2017, October 26). *Nonverbal communication with adolescents.* Matthew McNutt. https://matthewmcnutt.com/2017/10/26/nonverbal-communication-with-adolescents/

Morin, A. (2019a, July 7). *Activities to increase emotional vocabulary.* ThoughtCo. https://www.thoughtco.com/activities-to-increase-emotional-vocabulary-2086623

Morin, A. (2019b, September 17). *How to teach time management skills to teens.* Verywell Family. https://www.verywellfamily.com/teaching-time-management-skills-to-teens-2608794

Morin, A. (2020, June 11). *How to give your teen constructive criticism.* Verywell Family. https://www.verywell

family.com/how-to-give-your-teen-criticicism-4086439

Morin, A. (2021a, January 31). *Steps to good decision making skills for teens.* Verywell Family. https://www.verywellfamily.com/steps-to-good-decision-making-skills-for-teens-2609104

Morin, A. (2021b, February 27). *8 ways to teach teens anger management skills.* Verywell Family. https://www.verywellfamily.com/teach-teens-anger-management-skills-2609114

Morin, A. M. (2019, August 8). *10 strategies to limit your teen's screen time.* Verywell Family. https://www.verywellfamily.com/strategies-limit-your-teens-screen-time-2608915

Mullally, V. (2022, April 8). *How to create a safe space so your teen will talk.* MyKidsTime. https://www.mykidstime.com/for-parents/how-to-create-a-safe-space-so-your-teen-will-talk/

Nace, S. (2023, May 30). *Preparing for an empty nest.* PennState Extension. https://extension.psu.edu/preparing-for-an-empty-nest

9 questions to ask your teens to get to know their hearts. (2023, August 7). All Pro Dad. https://www.allprodad.com/9-questions-to-ask-your-teen/

Nurturing the parent-teenager relationship: Building bonds that last. (2023, June 2). *Tod Augusta Scott Family Therapy.* https://todascott.com/blog/parent-teen-relationships/

Paris, D. (2023, October 12). *Parents guide to financial literacy for kids & teens.* MyDOH. https://www.mydoh.ca/learn/money-101/money-basics/parents-guide-to-financial-literacy-for-kids-teens/

Paulus, N. (2023, December 8). *Teens' guide to building a strong personal finance foundation.* MoneyGeek.com. https://www.moneygeek.com/financial-planning/personal-finance-for-teens/

Peer pressure or influence: Pre-teens and teenagers. (2021, November 3). Raising Children Network. https://raisingchildren.net.au/teens/behaviour/peers-friends-trends/peer-influence

Pellissier, H. (2020, October 29). *9 tips for keeping the peace.* Parenting. https://www.greatschools.org/gk/articles/9-tips-teaching-kids-forgiveness-keeping-peace/

Peper, J. S., & Dahl, R. E. (2013). The teenage brain. *Current Directions in Psychological Science, 22*(2), 134–139. https://doi.org/10.1177/0963721412473755

Pierce, R. (2023, October 18). 13 practical time management skills to teach teens. *Life Skills Advocate.*

https://lifeskillsadvocate.com/blog/13-practical-time-management-skills-to-teach-teens/

Pontz, E. (2022, December 6). *Creating safe boundaries for teens to push against.* Center for Parent and Teen Communication. https://parentandteen.com/creating-safe-boundaries/

Powell, K. (2006). How does the teenage brain work? *Nature, 442*(7105), 865–867. https://doi.org/10.1038/442865a

Preparing for college & career success: What every teen and parent should know. (2023, April 18). Boys & Girls Clubs of America. https://www.bgca.org/news-stories/2023/April/preparing-for-college-and-career-success-what-every-teen-and-parent-should-know

Price, C. (2020, August 24). *Strengthening your teen's social and conversation abilities.* Hey Sigmund. https://www.heysigmund.com/strengthening-teens-social-conversation-abilities/

Problem solving - Self-help CBT techniques - Every mind matters. (n.d.). nhs.uk. https://www.nhs.uk/every-mind-matters/mental-wellbeing-tips/self-help-cbt-techniques/problem-solving/

6 ways to overcome negative thinking. (n.d.). *Bakersfield Behavioral Healthcare Hospital.*https://www.bakersfield

behavioral.com/blog/overcoming-negative-thinking

Quevedo, A. (2019, October). *Talking to your teen about sensitive issues.* Sutter Health. https://www.sutterhealth. org/health/parenting-preteens-teens/parenting-tips/ talking-to-your-teen

Relationship Matters. (2022, March 30). *Parent adolescent mediation.* Relationship Matters. https://relation shipmatters.com.au/services/parent-adolescent- mediation/

Resilience in pre-teens and teenagers. (2021, July 12). Raising Children Network. https://raisingchildren.net. au/pre-teens/development/social-emotional-develop ment/resilience-in-teens

Roudabush, C. (2019, April 9). *Why spending quality time with your children is important.* SDSU Extension. https:// extension.sdstate.edu/why-spending-quality-time- your-children-important

Roy Chowdhury, M. (2019, August 13). *Emotional regulation: 6 key skills to regulate emotions.* PositivePsycholo- gy.com. https://positivepsychology.com/emotion- regulation/

Set realistic boundaries with your teenager. (n.d.). ReachOut Parents. https://parents.au.reachout.com/ skills-to-build/connecting-and-communicating/

things-to-try-building-trust/set-realistic-boundaries-with-your-teenager

Shackney, R. (2023, January 14). Empathize with your teen with the DBT validation skill. *Rebekah Shackney LCSW.* https://rebekahshackney.com/blog/2023/1/14/eacxvk78ackxauqaligv2l49h9ciq9

Shannonhouse, G. (2023, July 7). Dealing with teenage rebellion and defiance. *Trails Carolina.* https://trailscarolina.com/blog/dealing-teenage-rebellion-defiance/

Sharkey, S. (2023, May 7). *Financial literacy for teenagers: Key money tips for teens.* Clever Girl Finance. https://www.clevergirlfinance.com/financial-literacy-for-teenagers/

Sibling fighting: pre-teens and teenagers. (2021, November 3). Raising Children Network. https://raisingchildren.net.au/pre-teens/behaviour/sibling-fights/sibling-fighting

Sippl, A. (2023, December 13). What household skills does your teen need to know? *Life Skills Advocate.* https://lifeskillsadvocate.com/blog/what-household-skills-does-your-teen-need-to-know/

The skill of active listening. (2018, October 26). The Center for Parenting Education. https://centerforpar

entingeducation.org/library-of-articles/healthy-communication/the-skill-of-listening/

Smith, M. (2023a, June 21). *Parent's guide to teen depression.* HelpGuide.org. https://www.helpguide.org/articles/depression/parents-guide-to-teen-depression.htm

Smith, M., MA. (2023b, June 21). *Dealing with teen depression.* HelpGuide.org. https://www.helpguide.org/articles/depression/teenagers-guide-to-depression.htm

Smith, M., Segal, J., Robinson, L., & Shubin, J. (2023, October 5). *Improving emotional intelligence (EQ).* HelpGuide.org. https://www.helpguide.org/articles/mental-health/emotional-intelligence-eq.htm

Social media benefits and risks: pre-teens and teenagers. (2022, October 14). Raising Children Network. https://raisingchildren.net.au/teens/entertainment-technology/digital-life/social-media

Sosso, J. (2022, September 6). *Tips for enjoying your empty nest.* Mayo Clinic Health System. https://www.mayoclinichealthsystem.org/hometown-health/speaking-of-health/how-you-can-enjoy-the-empty-nest

Spear, S. (2023, August 11). *Dear parents: This is what I need from you during these hard teen years.* parentingteensandtweens.com. https://parentingteensandtweens.com/5-tips-to-be-a-safe-space-for-your-teens/

Staff, N. A. (2022, July 14). *Effects of social media on teenagers*. Newport Academy. https://www.newporta cademy.com/resources/well-being/effect-of-social-media-on-teenagers/

Sticco, M. (2023, March 3). *Why it's important to spend time with your teenager*. Upstream Parent. https://www.upstreamparent.org/?p=2193

Stress management and teens. (2019, January). American Academy of Child and Adolescent Psychiatry. https://www.aacap.org/AACAP/Families_and_Youth/Facts_for_Families/FFF-Guide/Helping-Teenagers-With-Stress-066.aspx

Suraliya, S. (2023, March 2). *10 most effective emotional regulation techniques*. Your Mental Health Pal. https://yourmentalhealthpal.com/emotional-regulation-techniques/

Swenson, S. J., Ho, G. W., Budhathoki, C., Belcher, H. M. E., Tucker, S., Miller, K., & Gross, D. (2016). Parents' use of praise and criticism in a sample of young children seeking mental health services. *Journal of Pediatric Health Care, 30*(1), 49–56. https://doi.org/10.1016/j.pedhc.2015.09.010

Teenage screen time and digital technology use: Tips for balance. (2022, October 28). Raising Children Network. https://raisingchildren.net.au/teens/entertainment-technology/screen-time-healthy-screen-use/healthy-screen-time-teens

Teens and social media use: What's the impact? (2022, February 26). Mayo Clinic. https://www.mayoclinic.org/healthy-lifestyle/tween-and-teen-health/in-depth/teens-and-social-media-use/art-20474437

10 ways to teach your children how to forgive. (2023, August 8). All Pro Dad. https://www.allprodad.com/10-ways-to-teach-your-children-how-to-forgive/

13 ways to overcome negative thought patterns. (2016, May 9). Forbes. https://www.forbes.com/sites/forbescoachescouncil/2016/05/09/13-coaches-explain-how-to-overcome-negative-thought-patterns/

Thomas-Odia, I. (2023, June 24). *Teach your child forgiveness skills.* The Guardian Nigeria News. https://guardian.ng/guardian-woman/teach-your-child-forgiveness-skills/

13 ways to overcome negative thought patterns. (2021, November 15). *Stonewater Recovery.* https://www.stonewaterrecovery.com/adolescent-treatment-blog/3-ways-hormones-impact-teen-mental-health?hs_amp=true

Tips for having a difficult conversation with your teen. (n.d.). ReachOut Parents. https://parents.au.reachout.

com/skills-to-build/connecting-and-communicating/things-to-try-effective-communication/tips-for-having-a-difficult-conversation-with-your-teen

Tiret, H. (2015, May 11). *Helping teens learn independence and responsibility – Part 1*. MSU Extension. https://www.canr.msu.edu/news/helping_teens_learn_independence_and_responsibility_part_1

VanDuzer, T. (2021, February 24). 13 time management techniques for teens. *Student-Tutor Education Blog*. https://student-tutor.com/blog/time-management-techniques-for-teens/

Walker, T. (2022, October 26). 10 tips to prepare teens for their high school career. *TeenLife*. https://www.teenlife.com/blog/10-tips-to-prepare-teens-for-their-high-school-career/

Walsh, G. (2022). *Creating a safe space to talk to teens*. Familyfriendlyhq.ie. https://www.familyfriendlyhq.ie/amp/secondary-school/creating-a-safe-space-to-talk-to-teens-30239/

Welker, G. (2021, September 15). 4 keys to mindful communication with teens. *Inward Bound Mindfulness*. https://ibme.com/blog/mindful-communication-with-teens/

West, J. (2018, June 11). *Using appreciative inquiry in parent/teen mediation*. Academy of Professional Family Mediators. https://apfmnet.org/appreciative-inquiry-parent-teen-mediation/

What is cognitive behavioral therapy? (2017, July 31). American Psychological Association. https://www.apa.org/ptsd-guideline/patients-and-families/cognitive-behavioral

What is emotional intelligence and how does it apply to the workplace? (n.d.). Mental Health America. https://mhanational.org/what-emotional-intelligence-and-how-does-it-apply-workplace

Why active listening is important in parent-child relationships. (2022, March 1). The Family Centre. https://www.familycentre.org/news/post/why-active-listening-is-important-in-parent-child-relationships

Willard, C. (2023, May 18). *5 ways to help teens engage in mindfulness sessions*. Mindful. https://www.mindful.org/5-ways-to-help-teens-engage-in-mindfulness-sessions/

Williams, J. A. (2023, August 28). Positive parenting solutions: How to set healthy boundaries and consequences for teenage rebellion. *Heartmanity Blog*. https://blog.heartmanity.com/how-to-set-healthy-boundaries-and-consequences-for-teenage-rebellion?hs_amp=true

Made in the USA
Monee, IL
26 March 2024

55812770R00114